Elevate Your Home, Wardrobe with Crochet

With 84 Stunning Year Round Decorations and Clothing Pieces

Dom N Youri

THIS BOOK BELONGS TO
The Library of

....

....

Thanks ever so much to each of my cherished readers for investing the time to read this book!

I know you could have picked from many other books, but you chose this one. So, a big thanks for reading all the way to the end. If you enjoyed this book or received value from it, I'd like to ask you for a favor. Please take a few minutes to **post an honest and heartfelt review on *Amazon.com.*** Your support does make a difference and helps to benefit other people.

Thanks!

The trademarks that are used are without any consent, and the publication of the trademark is without permission or backing by the trademark owner. All trademarks and brands within this book are for clarifying purposes only and are the owned by the owners themselves, not affiliated with this document.

Table of Contents

SUMMARY

What is Crochet?: Crochet is a craft that involves creating fabric by interlocking loops of yarn or thread using a crochet hook. It is a versatile and popular form of needlework that can be used to create a wide range of items, from clothing and accessories to home decor and toys.

The process of crocheting begins with a slip knot, which is created by making a loop with the yarn and pulling the end through. The slip knot is then placed on the crochet hook, and additional loops are created by wrapping the yarn around the hook and pulling it through the existing loops. This creates a chain stitch, which serves as the foundation for most crochet projects.

Once the chain stitch is established, various crochet stitches can be used to create different patterns and textures. Some common stitches include the single crochet, double crochet, and treble crochet. These stitches are created by inserting the hook into specific loops of the previous row and pulling the yarn through to create new loops.

Crochet patterns typically consist of a combination of different stitches and techniques, which are repeated in a specific sequence to create the desired design. Patterns can range from simple and beginner-friendly to complex and intricate, depending on the skill level of the crocheter.

One of the advantages of crochet is its portability and accessibility. Unlike other forms of needlework, crochet requires minimal equipment and can be done almost anywhere. All you need is a crochet hook, some yarn, and a pattern to get started. Additionally, crochet is a relatively quick craft, allowing for the creation of projects in a relatively short amount of time.

Crochet is also a highly customizable craft, as it allows for the use of different types of yarn, colors, and stitch combinations. This means that each crocheted item can be unique and personalized to the individual's taste and style.

In addition to its creative and artistic aspects, crochet also offers a range of practical benefits. Crocheted items can be warm, durable, and functional, making them ideal for clothing and accessories such as hats, scarves, and blankets. Crochet can also be used to create decorative items for the home, such as doilies, pillow covers, and wall hangings.

Overall, crochet is a versatile and enjoyable craft that offers endless possibilities for creativity and self-expression. Whether you are a beginner or an experienced crocheter, there is always something new to learn and create in the world of crochet.

The Timeless Appeal of Handmade Creations in Crochet: Crochet, the art of creating fabric by interlocking loops of yarn or thread using a crochet hook, has been a beloved craft for centuries. Despite the advent of modern technology and mass production, the timeless appeal of handmade creations in crochet continues to captivate people of all ages and backgrounds.

One of the reasons why crochet has stood the test of time is its versatility. From delicate doilies and intricate lacework to cozy blankets and stylish garments, the possibilities are endless. The ability to create unique and personalized items is a major draw for many crochet enthusiasts. Whether it's a handmade baby blanket for a newborn or a one-of-a-kind scarf for a loved one, the sentimental value attached to these handmade creations cannot be replicated by store-bought items.

Furthermore, the process of crocheting itself is a therapeutic and meditative experience. As the crochet hook glides through the loops, the repetitive motions can help calm the mind and reduce stress. Many people find solace in the rhythmic nature of crochet, allowing them to unwind and focus on the present moment. In a fast-paced world filled with digital distractions, the act of creating something tangible with one's own hands can be incredibly rewarding.

Another reason why handmade crochet creations hold such appeal is the connection to tradition and heritage. Crochet has a rich history, with roots dating back to the 19th century. Passed down through generations, the craft has been a way for families to bond and preserve their cultural heritage. By continuing to create handmade crochet items, individuals can pay homage to their ancestors and keep these traditions alive.

In addition to the emotional and cultural significance, there are practical benefits to choosing handmade crochet creations. Handmade items are often of higher quality compared to mass-produced goods. Crafters take pride in their work and pay attention to every detail, ensuring that each stitch is perfect. This attention to detail results in durable and long-lasting items that can be cherished for years to come.

Moreover, supporting handmade crochet creations also means supporting small businesses and independent artisans. In a world dominated by big corporations, buying handmade allows consumers to directly support individuals who pour their heart and soul into their craft. By purchasing a handmade crochet item, customers are not only acquiring a unique and beautiful piece, but they are also contributing to the livelihood of a passionate artist.

In conclusion, the timeless appeal of handmade creations in crochet lies in their versatility, therapeutic nature, connection to tradition, and practical benefits.

Understanding Crochet Tools and Materials: Crochet is a popular craft that involves creating fabric by interlocking loops of yarn or thread using a crochet hook. To successfully engage in this craft, it is essential to have a good understanding of the various crochet tools and materials that are used.

One of the most important tools in crochet is the crochet hook. These hooks come in various sizes, ranging from small to large, and are made from different materials such as aluminum, plastic, or wood. The size of the crochet hook determines the size of the stitches and ultimately the size of the finished project. It is important to choose the right size hook for the yarn or thread being used to ensure that the stitches are neither too tight nor too loose.

Another essential tool in crochet is a pair of scissors. These are used to cut the yarn or thread when changing colors or finishing a project. It is important to have a sharp pair of scissors that can easily cut through the yarn without fraying or damaging it.

Yarn or thread is the main material used in crochet. There are countless options available when it comes to choosing yarn, including different fibers, weights, and colors. The type of yarn used can greatly affect the look and feel of the finished project. For beginners, it is recommended to start with a medium-weight yarn in a light color, as it is easier to work with and mistakes are less noticeable.

In addition to yarn, other materials that may be used in crochet include buttons, beads, and ribbons. These embellishments can be added to projects to enhance their appearance and add a personal touch. It is important to choose materials that are compatible with the yarn being used and that can withstand the wear and tear of everyday use.

To keep track of stitches and patterns, it is helpful to have a set of stitch markers. These small, removable markers are placed on the stitches to mark specific points in the pattern. They can be used to indicate the beginning of a round, the location of a stitch increase or decrease, or any other important points in the pattern. Stitch markers come in various shapes and sizes, and it is important to choose ones that are easy to use and do not snag the yarn.

Lastly, a tapestry needle is an essential tool for finishing crochet projects. This needle has a large eye and a blunt tip, making it easy to weave in loose ends and sew pieces together.

Learning the Fundamental Crochet Stitches: Learning the fundamental crochet stitches is an essential step for anyone interested in mastering the art of crochet. Crochet is a versatile craft that allows you to create beautiful and intricate designs using just a hook and yarn. Whether you're a beginner or have some experience with crochet, understanding and practicing the fundamental stitches is crucial for building a strong foundation in this craft.

The first stitch that every crocheter should learn is the chain stitch. This stitch forms the foundation of most crochet projects and is used to create a starting row or to add length to a project. The chain stitch is created by making a loop with the yarn and pulling it through the loop on the hook. It is a simple stitch that is easy to learn and master.

The next stitch to learn is the single crochet stitch. This stitch is commonly used in crochet projects and creates a tight and dense fabric. To make a single crochet stitch, you insert the hook into the next stitch, yarn over, and pull the yarn through the stitch. Then, yarn over again and pull through both loops on the hook. This stitch is great for creating solid and sturdy pieces, such as blankets or scarves.

Another important stitch to learn is the double crochet stitch. This stitch is taller than the single crochet stitch and creates a looser and more open fabric. To make a double crochet stitch, you yarn over, insert the hook into the next stitch, yarn over again, and pull the yarn through the stitch. Then, yarn over once more and pull through the first two loops on the hook. Finally, yarn over again and pull through the remaining two loops on the hook. The double crochet stitch is commonly used in projects that require more drape, such as shawls or garments.

Once you have mastered the chain, single crochet, and double crochet stitches, you can move on to more advanced stitches, such as the half double crochet, treble crochet, and shell stitch. These stitches add texture and complexity to your crochet projects and allow you to create unique and intricate designs.

Learning the fundamental crochet stitches is not only important for creating beautiful and well-structured crochet pieces, but it also opens up a world of possibilities for your creativity. With these stitches in your repertoire, you can experiment with different yarns, colors, and patterns to create one-of-a-kind crochet creations.

In conclusion, learning the fundamental crochet stitches is a crucial step in becoming a skilled crocheter.

Reading and Understanding Crochet Patterns: Reading and understanding crochet patterns is an essential skill for anyone interested in the art of crochet. Crochet patterns are like a roadmap that guides you through the process of creating a specific crochet project. They provide detailed instructions on the stitches to use, the number of stitches to make, and the order in which to make them.

To begin reading a crochet pattern, it is important to familiarize yourself with the abbreviations and symbols commonly used in crochet patterns. These abbreviations and symbols represent different stitches and techniques. For example, "ch" stands for chain stitch, "sc" stands for single crochet, and "dc" stands for double crochet. By understanding these abbreviations, you can easily follow the instructions in the pattern.

Once you are familiar with the abbreviations, the next step is to understand the structure of the pattern. Crochet patterns typically start with a list of materials needed for the project, followed by the gauge, which is the number of stitches and rows per inch that you should aim for. The pattern will then provide a set of instructions for each row or round, specifying the stitches to be made and any increases or decreases that need to be done.

It is important to read the pattern carefully and thoroughly before starting your project. Take note of any special instructions or stitch combinations that may be used. Some patterns may also include charts or diagrams to help visualize the pattern. These charts can be especially helpful for complex stitch patterns or when working with color changes.

As you work through the pattern, it is important to keep track of your progress. You can use stitch markers or a row counter to help you keep count of your stitches and rows. This will ensure that your project turns out the correct size and shape as specified in the pattern.

If you come across any unfamiliar stitches or techniques while reading a pattern, don't be afraid to seek help. There are numerous online resources, tutorial videos, and crochet communities where you can find guidance and support. Additionally, practicing with simpler patterns before tackling more complex ones can help build your confidence and understanding of crochet patterns.

In conclusion, reading and understanding crochet patterns is a skill that can be developed with practice and patience. By familiarizing yourself with the abbreviations, structure, and instructions in crochet patterns, you can confidently create beautiful crochet projects. So grab your crochet hook, yarn, and a pattern, and let your creativity flow!

Mastering Color Changes and Textures of Crochet: Mastering Color Changes and Textures of Crochet is a comprehensive guide that delves into the intricacies of manipulating colors and creating various textures in crochet projects. Whether you are a beginner or an experienced crocheter, this book will provide you with the knowledge and techniques to take your crochet skills to the next level.

The book begins by introducing the fundamentals of color theory and how it applies to crochet. You will learn about the color wheel, color schemes, and how to choose the right colors for your projects. The author explains how to create harmonious color combinations and how to use contrasting colors to make your crochet pieces pop.

Next, the book explores different techniques for changing colors in crochet. You will learn how to seamlessly transition from one color to another, whether it's for stripes, color blocks, or intricate color patterns. The author provides step-by-step instructions and helpful tips to ensure that your color changes are smooth and professional-looking.

In addition to color changes, this book also delves into the world of crochet textures. You will learn how to create a variety of textures, such as ribbing, cables, popcorn stitches, and more. The author explains the techniques behind each texture and provides patterns and examples to help you practice and master them.

Throughout the book, the author includes detailed photographs and illustrations to visually guide you through each step. The instructions are clear and concise, making it easy for even beginners to follow along. The book also includes helpful tips and troubleshooting advice to address common challenges that crocheters may encounter when working with colors and textures.

Whether you want to create vibrant blankets, textured scarves, or intricate garments, Mastering Color Changes and Textures of Crochet will equip you with the skills and knowledge to bring your crochet projects to life. With practice and experimentation, you will be able to confidently incorporate color changes and textures into your crochet designs, adding depth and visual interest to your creations.

Overall, this book is a valuable resource for anyone looking to expand their crochet skills and explore the creative possibilities of color changes and textures. Whether you are a hobbyist or aspire to become a professional crocheter, this book will inspire and empower you to create beautiful and unique crochet pieces that showcase your creativity and craftsmanship.

Understanding Gauge and Adjusting Patterns of Crochet:

Crocheting is a popular craft that involves creating fabric by interlocking loops of yarn or thread using a crochet hook. One important aspect of crocheting is understanding gauge, which refers to the number of stitches and rows per inch in a crochet pattern. Gauge is crucial because it determines the size and fit of the finished project.

When starting a crochet project, it is essential to check the gauge specified in the pattern. The gauge is usually given in terms of the number of stitches and rows needed to achieve a specific measurement, such as 4 inches by 4 inches. To determine if your gauge matches the pattern's gauge, you need to crochet a swatch.

To crochet a swatch, you should use the same yarn and hook size specified in the pattern. Start by chaining a few stitches, then work the specified stitch pattern for a few rows. Once you have completed the swatch, measure it using a ruler or a gauge tool. Count the number of stitches and rows within the specified measurement area and compare it to the pattern's gauge.

If your swatch matches the pattern's gauge, congratulations! You can proceed with confidence, knowing that your finished project will have the correct size and fit. However, if your gauge is off, adjustments need to be made.

If your swatch has fewer stitches and rows than the pattern's gauge, it means your stitches are too loose. To tighten your stitches, you can try using a smaller hook size or adjusting your tension. Tension refers to how tightly you hold the yarn while crocheting. Experiment with different tension levels until you achieve the desired gauge.

On the other hand, if your swatch has more stitches and rows than the pattern's gauge, it means your stitches are too tight. To loosen your stitches, you can try using a larger hook size or adjusting your tension to be more relaxed. Again, practice different tension levels until you achieve the correct gauge.

It is crucial to note that changing the hook size or tension can affect the overall appearance and drape of the fabric. Therefore, it is essential to make adjustments gradually and test them on your swatch before applying them to your entire project.

In some cases, adjusting the hook size or tension may not be enough to achieve the correct gauge. If this happens, you may need to consider using a different yarn weight or adjusting the pattern itself.

Tips for Creating Neat and Consistent Stitches of Crochet: Crocheting is a popular and enjoyable craft that allows you to create beautiful and intricate designs using just a hook and yarn. One of the key elements to achieving a polished and professional-looking crochet project is creating neat and consistent stitches. Whether you're a beginner or an experienced crocheter, here are some tips to help you improve your stitch quality and create stunning crochet pieces.

1. Choose the Right Yarn and Hook Size: The type of yarn and hook size you use can greatly impact the appearance of your stitches. Thicker yarns and larger hooks will result in larger and looser stitches, while thinner yarns and smaller hooks will create smaller and tighter stitches. Experiment with different combinations to find the right balance for your desired project.

2. Maintain Tension: Consistent tension is crucial for achieving neat and even stitches. Tension refers to the amount of pressure you apply to the yarn as you crochet. If your tension is too tight, your stitches will be small and difficult to work with. On the other hand, if your tension is too loose, your stitches will be uneven and sloppy. Practice maintaining a steady tension by keeping your yarn taut but not overly tight.

3. Practice Proper Stitch Placement: Each crochet stitch has a specific placement that determines its height and appearance. Pay close attention to where you insert your hook and how you pull the yarn through to create each stitch. Crocheting into the correct loops and spaces will result in clean and uniform stitches. Take your time to understand the anatomy of each stitch and practice until you can consistently place them correctly.

4. Use Stitch Markers: Stitch markers are invaluable tools for keeping track of your stitches, especially when working on complex patterns. They can help you identify the beginning and end of each round or row, ensuring that your stitch count remains consistent. By using stitch markers, you can avoid accidental increases or decreases and maintain the overall shape and structure of your project.

5. Block Your Finished Pieces: Blocking is a technique used to shape and smooth out your crochet work. It involves wetting or steaming your

finished piece and then pinning it into the desired shape and size. Blocking can help even out any uneven stitches, open up lacework, and give your project a more polished and professional look. Follow the specific blocking instructions for your chosen yarn to achieve the best results.

6. Practice, Practice, Practice: Like any skill, improving your crochet stitches requires practice.

Care, Repair, and Preservation of Crochet Items: The care, repair, and preservation of crochet items is essential to ensure their longevity and maintain their beauty. Crochet items, whether they are delicate doilies, cozy blankets, or fashionable garments, require special attention and care to keep them in pristine condition.

When it comes to caring for crochet items, the first step is to understand the materials used. Crochet can be made from a variety of fibers, including cotton, wool, acrylic, and blends. Each type of fiber has its own specific care requirements. For example, cotton can usually be machine washed and dried, while wool may need to be hand washed and laid flat to dry. It is important to read the care instructions provided by the yarn manufacturer and follow them accordingly.

To prevent damage, it is advisable to store crochet items properly when they are not in use. This includes folding them neatly or rolling them up, depending on the item's size and shape. It is best to store crochet items in a clean, dry place away from direct sunlight, as exposure to sunlight can cause fading and weakening of the fibers over time.

Regular cleaning is also crucial for maintaining crochet items. However, it is important to be gentle when washing them to avoid stretching or distorting the stitches. Hand washing is often the safest method, using a mild detergent and lukewarm water. Avoid scrubbing or wringing the item, as this can cause damage. Instead, gently squeeze out excess water and lay the item flat on a clean towel to dry.

Repairing crochet items is a skill that can come in handy when accidents happen or wear and tear occurs. Small tears or loose stitches can be fixed by carefully weaving in the loose ends or using a crochet hook to re-stitch the damaged area. For more extensive damage, such as large holes or unraveling, it may be necessary to unravel the affected section and re-crochet it. This requires some skill and patience, but with practice, it can be a rewarding way to restore a beloved crochet item.

Preserving crochet items for future generations involves taking extra precautions. If an item is particularly delicate or valuable, it may be worth considering storing it in acid-free tissue paper or a cotton bag to protect it from dust and pests. Additionally, periodically inspecting the item for any signs of damage or deterioration can help catch any issues early on and prevent further damage.

Washing and Caring for Crochet Items: Washing and caring for crochet items is essential to maintain their quality and prolong their lifespan. Crochet items, such as clothing, accessories, and home decor, require special attention due to their delicate nature. By following a few simple steps, you can ensure that your crochet items remain in excellent condition for years to come.

Firstly, it is important to read and follow the care instructions provided by the manufacturer or the crochet pattern designer. These instructions may vary depending on the type of yarn used, the stitch pattern, and any additional embellishments or decorations on the item. Care instructions may include specific washing temperatures, recommended detergents, and whether the item can be machine washed or should be hand washed.

When it comes to washing crochet items, it is generally recommended to hand wash them to prevent any damage or distortion. Fill a basin or sink with lukewarm water and add a mild detergent specifically designed for delicate fabrics. Gently submerge the crochet item in the water and swish it around to ensure that the detergent reaches all parts of the item. Avoid rubbing or scrubbing the crochet item, as this can cause it to lose its shape or become tangled.

After soaking the crochet item for a few minutes, drain the soapy water and refill the basin or sink with clean lukewarm water. Rinse the item thoroughly, making sure to remove all traces of detergent. Repeat this rinsing process if necessary until the water runs clear. Avoid wringing or twisting the crochet item, as this can stretch or damage the fibers. Instead, gently squeeze out excess water by pressing the item between your hands or rolling it in a clean towel.

Once the excess water has been removed, reshape the crochet item to its original form. Lay it flat on a clean, dry towel or on a drying rack, making sure to arrange it in the correct shape and dimensions. Avoid hanging crochet items to dry, as this can cause them to stretch or lose their shape. Allow the item to air dry completely, which may take several hours or even overnight, depending on the thickness of the yarn and the size of the item.

In addition to washing, it is important to store crochet items properly to prevent any damage. Avoid folding or creasing the items, as this can create permanent lines or wrinkles. Instead, store them flat in a clean, dry place, such as a drawer or a storage box.

Repairing Damaged Crochet Pieces: When it comes to repairing damaged crochet pieces, there are several steps and techniques that can be employed to restore the item to its original condition. Whether it's a beloved heirloom or a cherished handmade creation, taking the time to repair damaged crochet pieces can not only extend their lifespan but also preserve the sentimental value they hold.

The first step in repairing damaged crochet pieces is to assess the extent of the damage. This involves carefully examining the piece and identifying any areas that require attention. Common issues that may need to be addressed include unraveling or broken stitches, holes, frayed edges, or loose threads. By thoroughly inspecting the crochet piece, you can determine the best course of action for repairing it.

Once the damage has been assessed, the next step is to gather the necessary materials and tools for the repair. This may include crochet hooks in various sizes, matching yarn or thread, a tapestry needle, scissors, and any additional embellishments or accessories that may be required. It's important to ensure that the materials chosen closely match the original piece in terms of color, texture, and weight to achieve a seamless repair.

The actual repair process will vary depending on the specific damage that needs to be addressed. For unraveling or broken stitches, it may be necessary to carefully pick up the loops and rework the stitches using a crochet hook. This requires a steady hand and a good understanding of crochet techniques. For holes or frayed edges, a technique called "darning" can be used, which involves weaving in new yarn or thread to fill in the gaps and reinforce the damaged area.

In some cases, it may be necessary to replace entire sections of the crochet piece if the damage is too extensive to repair. This can be done by carefully removing the damaged section and crocheting a new piece to seamlessly blend with the existing work. This technique requires a high level of skill and precision to ensure that the repaired section matches the original piece in terms of stitch pattern and tension.

Once the repair has been completed, it's important to block the crochet piece to help it regain its shape and ensure that the repaired area blends in with the rest of the piece. Blocking involves wetting the crochet piece, shaping it to the desired dimensions, and allowing it to dry flat. This helps to even out any tension discrepancies and gives the repaired area a polished finish.

In conclusion, repairing damaged crochet pieces requires careful assessment, the right materials and tools, and a good understanding of crochet techniques.

"Storing Crochet Creations Safely: When it comes to storing crochet creations safely, there are several important factors to consider. Crochet creations, whether they are blankets, garments, or accessories, require proper care and storage to ensure their longevity and prevent any damage. Here are some tips and guidelines to help you store your crochet creations effectively.

Firstly, it is crucial to clean your crochet creations before storing them. This involves washing or dry cleaning them, depending on the yarn and fiber used. Follow the care instructions provided with the yarn or consult a professional cleaner if you are unsure. Cleaning your crochet creations removes any dirt, oils, or stains that may have accumulated over time, preventing them from becoming permanent and potentially damaging the fibers.

Once your crochet creations are clean and dry, it is essential to choose the right storage containers. Opt for containers that are clean, dry, and free from any chemicals or odors that could transfer onto your crochet items. Clear plastic containers with tight-fitting lids are a popular choice as they allow you to easily see what is inside while providing protection from dust, insects, and moisture. Avoid using cardboard boxes or bags that can attract pests or allow moisture to seep in.

Before placing your crochet creations in the storage containers, it is advisable to add some additional protection. Acid-free tissue paper or clean cotton sheets can be used to wrap delicate or heirloom pieces, providing an extra layer of cushioning and preventing any potential snagging or tangling. For larger items such as blankets, folding them neatly and placing them in a cotton or muslin bag can help maintain their shape and protect them from dust.

When arranging your crochet creations in the storage containers, it is important to avoid overcrowding. Overstuffing the containers can lead to creasing, stretching, or distortion of the crochet items. Allow enough space for each piece to lay flat or hang freely, depending on its size and shape. If you are storing multiple items in one container, consider separating them with acid-free tissue paper or cotton sheets to prevent any friction or rubbing between them.

In addition to proper storage containers, it is crucial to choose an appropriate storage location. Ideally, the storage area should be cool, dry, and well-ventilated. Avoid areas that are prone to extreme temperature fluctuations, high humidity, or direct sunlight, as these conditions can cause damage to the fibers and colors of your crochet creations. Attics, basements, and garages are generally not recommended due to their fluctuating temperatures and potential for moisture.

Adapting and Customizing Crochet Patterns: Adapting and customizing crochet patterns is a skill that allows crocheters to create unique and personalized projects. Whether you want to modify an existing pattern to fit your specific needs or design your own pattern from scratch, this process requires a combination of creativity, problem-solving, and technical knowledge.

When it comes to adapting crochet patterns, there are several factors to consider. First, you need to assess the pattern itself and determine what changes you want to make. This could involve altering the size, adjusting the stitch count, changing the color scheme, or adding or removing elements. It's important to have a clear vision of what you want to achieve before you start making any modifications.

Next, you'll need to understand the construction of the pattern. This includes familiarizing yourself with the stitch techniques used, the stitch count and gauge, and any shaping or assembly instructions. By understanding how the pattern is structured, you can better identify where and how to make changes without compromising the overall design.

One of the most common modifications in crochet patterns is adjusting the size. This can be done by changing the hook size, yarn weight, or stitch count. For example, if you want to make a sweater larger, you may need to use a larger hook and increase the stitch count accordingly. Conversely, if you want to make a project smaller, you would use a smaller hook and decrease the stitch count.

Color customization is another way to personalize crochet patterns. You can experiment with different color combinations to create a unique look or match your personal style. This can be as simple as substituting one color for another or as complex as creating intricate colorwork patterns. By understanding color theory and how different colors interact, you can create visually appealing and harmonious designs.

Adding or removing elements from a pattern is another way to customize it. This could involve adding a border, embellishments, or additional motifs. Conversely, you may want to simplify a pattern by removing certain elements that you don't like or find unnecessary. This requires careful consideration of the pattern's structure and how the changes will affect the overall design.

Designing your own crochet pattern from scratch is the ultimate form of customization. This requires a deep understanding of crochet techniques, stitch combinations, and pattern construction. You'll need to sketch out your design, determine the stitch pattern, calculate the stitch count and gauge, and write clear instructions. This process can be challenging but also incredibly rewarding, as you have complete creative control over the final product.

Winter Crochet:
Wonderful Crochet Projects To Warm You And Your Loved Ones

Introduction

Sleigh bells are ringing, bells are jingling, and there are people singing in the streets. You don't know what it is, but it just seems as though people are nicer this time of the year. They are ready to hold the door open for you – they are ready to give a little more when they are standing in line, and they are ready to be a little nicer to those around them.

Suddenly, it doesn't matter so much that there are crowds in the streets or other people in line at the shopping mall. It doesn't matter that it is cold and snowy, or that you are going to have to wait a little longer to get things done. When it comes to the holidays, you are ready to set a lot aside for others.

This is the season of giving, and you want to enjoy every second of it – and you know one of the best ways to do that is by bundling up in your favorite style, and heading out to experience all the joys of the season.

When it comes to the holidays, you know that there are many different things you want to do and experience, and you want to do all of them feeling great. When you know you look good, you feel good, and you are going to do that by wearing your favorite – well – everything.

And what better way to know that you are going to get the custom fit than when you make it yourself? You'll get the perfect fit, you'll get the perfect color, and you'll get everything that you have been wanting in your winter wardrobe.

But where are you going to get these patterns? Where are you going to get these custom pieces that fit you just right in all the right places? Obviously, if you are going to get such a perfect thing, you are going to have to make it yourself.

And that's where this book comes in. In it, you are going to discover everything you need to create the perfect wardrobe no matter what you are looking for. This book is going to be your perfect inspiration, and with the dash of creativity you are going to add to the mix, you are going to end up with the perfect pieces no matter what.

Get ready to dive into a whole new world of fashion, and dive into this world with a whole new sense of style.

You know you want to, so what are you waiting for? You're brimming with creativity, so get ready to dive into a whole new world of fashion.

Let's get started.

The Projects

Pretty Kitty Cuffs

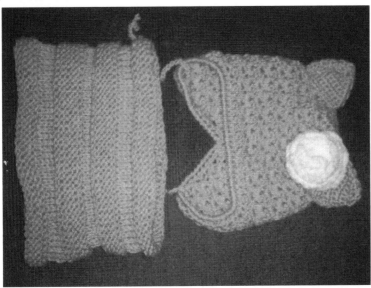

You will need 1 skein of yarn in the color of your choice and a size G crochet hook

You will also need a yarn needle and scissors.

For the hat:

Chain 4 and join with a slip stitch to form a ring. Single crochet in the center of this ring 8 times, and join with another slip stitch. Chain 1, turn, and single crochet across the row. Join with a slip stitch.

Chain 1, turn, and single crochet in the first stitch, then double crochet in the next stitch 2 times. Single crochet in the next stitch, then double crochet in the next stitch 2 times. Single crochet in the next stitch, then double crochet in the next stitch 2 times. Single crochet in the next stitch. Continue this around the row, and join with a slip stitch.

Chain 1, turn, and single crochet in the first stitch, then skip the next stitch. Single crochet in the next stitch, then skip the next stitch.

Repeat this around, then join with a slip stitch at the end.

Chain 1, turn, and single crochet in the first stitch, then double crochet in the next stitch 2 times. Single crochet in the next stitch, then double crochet in the next stitch 2 times. Single crochet in the next stitch, then double crochet in the next stitch 2 times. Single crochet in the next stitch. Continue this around the row, and join with a slip stitch.

Chain 1, turn, and single crochet in the first stitch, then skip the next stitch. Single crochet in the next stitch, then skip the next stitch. Repeat this around, then join with a slip stitch at the end.

You are going to measure as you go with this, working until the top of the hat reaches across the top of your head. Usually you are going to increase for about 12 rows. Next, you are going to fit the hat to your head.

Chain 1, turn, and single crochet in the first stitch, then skip the next 2 stitches. Single crochet in the next stitch, then skip the next 2 stitches. Repeat this around, then join with a slip stitch at the end.

Chain 1, turn, and single crochet in the first stitch, then double crochet in the next stitch 2 times. Single crochet in the next stitch, then double crochet in the next stitch 2 times. Single crochet in the next stitch, then double crochet in the next stitch 2 times. Single crochet in the next stitch. Continue this around the row, and join with a slip stitch.

Repeat until the hat fits your head, then finish with a border around the base.

For each of the ears you are going to chain 10 and skip the first stitch, single crocheting across the row and skipping the last stitch. Single crochet across the row. Chain 1, skip the first stitch, and single crochet across the row, skipping the last stitch. Repeat until you have a triangle. Repeat for the other ear.

Sew the ears in place, and tie off.

For the scarf:

Chain a length that is 2 feet long. Single crochet across the row. Chain 1, turn, and single crochet back to the beginning. Chain 1, turn, and single crochet across the row. Chain 1, turn, and single crochet back to the beginning. Chain 1, turn, and single crochet across the row. Chain 1, turn, and single crochet back to the beginning. Chain 1, turn, and single crochet across the row.

Chain 1, turn, and single crochet across the row in the front loop only. Chain 1, turn, and single crochet back to the beginning in the front loop only. Chain 1, turn, and single crochet across the row in the front loop only. Chain 1, turn, and single crochet back to the beginning in the front loop only.

Chain a length that is 2 feet long. Single crochet across the row. Chain 1, turn, and single crochet back to the beginning. Chain 1, turn, and single crochet across the row. Chain 1, turn, and single crochet back to the beginning. Chain 1, turn, and single crochet across the row. Chain 1, turn, and single crochet back to the beginning. Chain 1, turn, and single crochet across the row.

Chain 1, turn, and single crochet across the row in the front loop only. Chain 1, turn, and single crochet back to the beginning in the front loop only. Chain 1, turn, and single crochet across the row in the front loop only. Chain 1, turn, and single crochet back to the beginning in the front loop only.

Repeat until the scarf measure six inches thick. Tie off.

Take your yarn needle and sew up the ends, creating an eternity scarf. Tie off, and you are done!

That's A Wrap Scarf And Beanie Set

You will need 2 skeins of yarn in the color of your choice and a size J crochet hook

You will also need a yarn needle and scissors.

For the hat:

Chain 4 and join with a slip stitch to form a ring. Single crochet in the center of this ring 8 times, and join with another slip stitch. Chain 1, turn, and single crochet across the row. Join with a slip stitch.

Chain 1, turn, and single crochet in the first stitch, then double crochet in the next stitch 2 times. Single crochet in the next stitch, then double crochet in the next stitch 2 times. Single crochet in the next stitch, then double crochet in the next stitch 2 times. Single crochet in the next stitch. Continue this around the row, and join with a slip stitch.

Chain 1, turn, and single crochet in the first stitch, then skip the next stitch. Single crochet in the next stitch, then skip the next stitch. Repeat this around, then join with a slip stitch at the end.

Chain 1, turn, and single crochet in the first stitch, then double crochet in the next stitch 2 times. Single crochet in the next stitch, then double crochet in the next stitch 2 times. Single crochet in the next stitch, then double crochet in the next stitch 2 times. Single crochet in the next stitch. Continue this around the row, and join with a slip stitch.

Chain 1, turn, and single crochet in the first stitch, then skip the next stitch. Single crochet in the next stitch, then skip the next stitch. Repeat this around, then join with a slip stitch at the end.

You are going to measure as you go with this, working until the top of the hat reaches across the top of your head. Usually you are going to increase for about 12 rows. Next, you are going to fit the hat to your head.

Chain 1, turn, and single crochet in the first stitch, then skip the next 2 stitches. Single crochet in the next stitch, then skip the next 2 stitches. Repeat this around, then join with a slip stitch at the end.

Chain 1, turn, and single crochet in the first stitch, then double crochet in the next stitch 2 times. Single crochet in the next stitch, then double crochet in the next stitch 2 times. Single crochet in the next stitch, then double crochet in the next stitch 2 times. Single crochet in the next stitch. Continue this around the row, and join with a slip stitch.

Repeat until the hat fits your head, then finish with a border around the base.

Tie off.

For the scarf:

Chain a length that is 3 feet long.

Chain 2, turn, and double crochet back to the beginning. Chain 2, turn and double crochet across the row. Chain 2, turn, and double crochet back to the beginning. Chain 2, turn, and double crochet across the row. Chain 2, turn, and double crochet back to the beginning. Chain 2, turn, and double crochet across the row.

Chain 2, turn, and double crochet back to the beginning. Chain 2, turn and double crochet across the row. Chain 2, turn, and double crochet back to the beginning. Chain 2, turn, and double crochet across the row. Chain 2, turn, and double crochet back to the beginning. Chain 2, turn, and double crochet across the row.

Repeat until the scarf measure six inches thick. Tie off.

Take your yarn needle and sew up the ends, creating an eternity scarf. Tie off, and you are done!

Around the World Eternity Scarf

You will need 1 skein of yarn in the color of your choice and a size G crochet hook

You will also need a yarn needle and scissors.

Chain a length that is 4 feet long. Single crochet across the row. Chain 1, turn, and single crochet back to the beginning. Chain 1, turn, and single crochet across the row. Chain 1, turn, and single crochet back to the beginning. Chain 1, turn, and single crochet across the row. Chain 1, turn, and single crochet back to the beginning. Chain 1, turn, and single crochet across the row.

Chain 1, turn, and single crochet back to the beginning. Chain 1, turn, and single crochet across the row. Chain 1, turn, and single crochet back to the beginning. Chain 1, turn, and single crochet across the row. Chain 1, turn, and single crochet back to the beginning. Chain 1, turn, and single crochet across the row.

Repeat until the scarf measure six inches thick. Tie off.

Take your yarn needle and sew up the ends, creating an eternity scarf. Tie off, and you are done!

Magical Mermaid Cozy Blanket

You will need 2 or 3 skeins of yarn in the color of your choice and a size J crochet hook

You will also need a yarn needle and scissors.

Chain a length that is 8 feet long – larger or smaller to adjust the size of the tale. When this is folded in half, it is going to fit around you, so make sure it is roomie enough.

Single crochet across the row. Chain 1, turn, and single crochet back to the beginning. Chain 1, turn, and single crochet across the row. Chain 1, turn, and single crochet back to the beginning. Chain 1, turn, and single crochet across the row. Chain 1, turn, and single crochet back to the beginning. Chain 1, turn, and single crochet across the row.

Single crochet across the row. Chain 1, turn, and single crochet back to the beginning. Chain 1, turn, and single crochet across the row. Chain 1, turn, and single crochet back to the beginning. Chain 1, turn, and single crochet across the row. Chain 1, turn, and single crochet back to the beginning. Chain 1, turn, and single crochet across the row. Keep going until this measures from your chest down past your feet.

Tie off.

Now, you are going to make the tail.

Chain a length that is 5 feet long. Single crochet across the row. Chain 1, turn, and single crochet back to the beginning. Chain 1, turn, and single crochet across the row. Chain 1, turn, and single crochet back to the beginning. Chain 1, turn, and single crochet across the row. Chain 1, turn, and single crochet back to the beginning. Chain 1, turn, and single crochet across the row.

This is the tail, continue until you are happy with the size, then tie off.

To finish:

Sew up the side of the larger piece you have made, creating the tube. Once this is sewn, you are going to gather the base by feeding a piece of yarn around the opening and pulling it closed. Insert the smaller square into this opening, pulling it closed into the shape of the tail.

Sew this securely into the blanket, and form the shape of the mermaid tale. Tie off, and you are done!

Snowball Fight Christmas Gloves

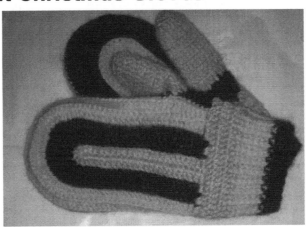

You will need scrap yarn or as many skeins of yarn in the colors of your choice and a size G crochet hook

You will also need a yarn needle and scissors.

Chain 1 length that is 4 inches long. Double crochet across the row, then down and across the bottom. Join with a slip stitch when you get back to the beginning. Chain 2, turn, and double crochet back up and around to the other side. Once again, you are going to join this with a slip stitch when you get back to the beginning.

You are going to follow this sequence until the size of your oval measures across your hand. Measure as you go to ensure you get the proper fit – and tie it off once you do.

Repeat this same sequence for the top of your hand, then once again for your thumbs.

Sew all the pieces together – the top and bottom of the hands, and the top and bottom of the thumbs – then you are going to sew the thumbs to the body of the mitten. Make sure there is enough room for your hands to slip in and out of the gloves easily, but not so easily that they fall off.

Next, you are going to make 3 strips for the cuff – make each one fit around your wrist, and follow the pattern for your glove.

Single crochet across the row. Chain 1, turn, and single crochet back to the beginning. Chain 1, turn, and single crochet across the row. Chain 1, turn, and single crochet back to the beginning. Tie off. Repeat for the next one. Do this 2 more times.

Sew each of these together and to the base of your glove – then repeat the process for the other hand. That's it! Your mittens are ready for anything!

The Diva Wrap

You will need 2 skeins of yarn in the color of your choice plus another skein in a different color for the trim and a size J crochet hook

You will also need a yarn needle and scissors.

For the body:

Measure from one shoulder to the other, then chain a length that is equal to this measurement. You are going to work the back of the piece first.

Chain 2, turn, and double crochet back to the beginning. Chain 2, turn and double crochet across the row. Chain 2, turn, and double crochet back to the beginning. Chain 2, turn, and double crochet across the row. Chain 2, turn, and double crochet back to the beginning. Chain 2, turn, and double crochet across the row.

Continue until it reaches from your shoulder to your hips.

Next, do the front of the piece. Starting at the bottom, chain a length that is equal to the first.

Chain 2, turn, and double crochet back to the beginning. Chain 2, turn and double crochet across the row. Chain 2, turn, and double crochet back to the beginning. Chain 2, turn, and double crochet across the row. Chain 2, turn, and double crochet back to the beginning. Chain 2, turn, and double crochet across the row.

When you reach your bust, start to move outward, creating the V.

Skip the first two stitches, then double crochet across the row. Double crochet back to the other side, once again skipping the last 2 stitches. Skip the first two stitches, then double crochet across the row. Double crochet back to the other side, once again skipping the last 2 stitches. Skip the first two stitches, then double crochet across the row. Double crochet back to the other side, once again skipping the last 2 stitches.

Continue until you reach the top of your shoulder.

For the other side, do the same thing, but using half the length.

Chain 2, turn, and double crochet back to the beginning. Chain 2, turn and double crochet across the row. Chain 2, turn, and double crochet back to the beginning. Chain 2, turn, and double crochet across the row. Chain 2, turn, and double crochet back to the beginning. Chain 2, turn, and double crochet across the row.

When you reach your bust, start to move outward, creating the V.

Skip the first two stitches, then double crochet across the row. Double crochet back to the other side, once again skipping the last 2 stitches. Skip the first two stitches, then double crochet across the row. Double crochet back to the other side, once again skipping the last 2 stitches. Skip the first two stitches, then double crochet across the row. Double crochet back to the other side, once again skipping the last 2 stitches.

Continue until you reach the top of your shoulder.

For the sleeves:

The sleeves are going to be made to fit your arm.

Chain 2, turn, and double crochet back to the beginning. Chain 2, turn and double crochet across the row. Chain 2, turn, and double crochet back to the beginning. Chain 2, turn, and double crochet across the row. Chain 2, turn, and double crochet back to the beginning. Chain 2, turn, and double crochet across the row.

Continue for the length you want your sleeves to be – this can be all the way down to your wrists, or stop at your elbows. When you are happy with the length, tie it off.

Repeat for the other side.

To finish:

Start by putting borders around all the open ends of your pieces. You want to have one end for both the cuffs, and a boarder around both the bottom and the neckline of your piece. You can do this with the same color or alternating colors – whichever you prefer.

Sew the front pieces to the back and up the sides, leaving a hole for the arms.

Next, you are going to sew the arms to the body, and snip off any of the loose ends. Add any ties you would like to have on the body of the piece, and tie the ends to keep them from unraveling. Make sure all is secure, and you are done!

Fireside Warmth Cardigan

You will need scrap yarn or as many skeins in as many colors as you would like to use – the equivalent of 3 skeins of yarn total. You will also need a size J crochet hook

You will also need a yarn needle and scissors.

For the body:

Measure from one shoulder to the other, then chain a length that is equal to this measurement. You are going to work the back of the piece first.

Chain 2, turn, and double crochet back to the beginning. Chain 2, turn and double crochet across the row. Chain 2, turn, and double crochet back to the beginning. Chain 2, turn, and double crochet across the row. Chain 2, turn, and double crochet back to the beginning. Chain 2, turn, and double crochet across the row.

You are going to make this as long as you want – but try to go down below your knees. You can use the photo as a reference guide for changing colors, or you can change according to your own preference. Do this for the front as well.

Next, do the front of the piece. Starting at the bottom, chain a length that is half the length of the first. Remember you are going to change colors according to the photo, or as you prefer.

When you reach your bust, start to move outward, creating the V.

Skip the first two stitches, then double crochet across the row. Double crochet back to the other side, once again skipping the last 2 stitches. Skip the first two stitches, then double crochet across the row. Double crochet back to the other side, once again skipping the last 2 stitches. Skip the first two stitches, then double crochet across the row. Double crochet back to the other side, once again skipping the last 2 stitches.

Continue until you reach the top of your shoulder.

For the other side, do the same thing, once again using half the length.

When you reach your bust, start to move outward, creating the V.

Skip the first two stitches, then double crochet across the row. Double crochet back to the other side, once again skipping the last 2 stitches. Skip the first two stitches, then double crochet across the row. Double crochet back to the other side, once again skipping the last 2 stitches. Skip the first two stitches, then double crochet across the row. Double crochet back to the other side, once again skipping the last 2 stitches.

Once again, continue until you reach the top of your shoulder.

For the sleeves:

The sleeves are going to be made to fit your arm.

Single crochet across the row. Chain 1, turn, and single crochet back to the beginning. Chain 1, turn, and single crochet across the row. Chain 1, turn, and single crochet back to the beginning. Chain 1, turn, and single crochet across the row. Chain 1, turn, and single crochet back to the beginning. Chain 1, turn, and single crochet across the row.

Sew the front pieces to the back and up the sides, leaving a hole for the arms.

Continue for the length you want your sleeves to be – this can be all the way down to your wrists, or stop at your elbows. When you are happy with the length, tie it off.

Repeat for the other side.

To finish:

Start by putting borders around all the open ends of your pieces. You want to have one end for both the cuffs, and a boarder around both the bottom and the neckline of your piece. You can do this with the same color or alternating colors – whichever you prefer.

Next, you are going to sew the arms to the body, and snip off any of the loose ends. Add any ties you would like to have on the body of the piece, and tie the ends to keep them from unraveling. Make sure all is secure, and you are done!

Holiday Happiness Winter Cardigan

You will need 2 skeins of yarn in the color of your choice and a size J crochet hook

You will also need a yarn needle and scissors.

For the body:

Measure from one shoulder to the other, then chain a length that is equal to this measurement. You are going to work the back of the piece first.

Single crochet across the row. Chain 1, turn, and single crochet back to the beginning. Chain 1, turn, and single crochet across the row. Chain 1, turn, and single crochet back to the beginning. Chain 1, turn, and single crochet across the row. Chain 1, turn, and single crochet back to the beginning. Chain 1, turn, and single crochet across the row. Continue until it reaches from your shoulder to your hem.

Next, do the front of the piece. Starting at the bottom, chain a length that is equal to the first.

Single crochet across the row. Chain 1, turn, and single crochet back to the beginning. Chain 1, turn, and single crochet across the row. Chain 1, turn, and single crochet back to the beginning. Chain 1, turn, and single crochet across the row. Chain 1, turn, and single crochet back to the beginning. Chain 1, turn, and single crochet across the row.

When you reach your bust, start to move outward, creating the V.

Skip the first two stitches, then double crochet across the row. Double crochet back to the other side, once again skipping the last 2 stitches. Skip the first two stitches, then double crochet across the row. Double crochet back to the other side, once again skipping the last 2 stitches. Skip the first two stitches, then double crochet across the row. Double crochet back to the other side, once again skipping the last 2 stitches.

Continue until you reach the top of your shoulder.

For the other side, do the same thing, but using half the length.

Single crochet across the row. Chain 1, turn, and single crochet back to the beginning. Chain 1, turn, and single crochet across the row. Chain 1, turn, and single crochet back to the beginning. Chain 1, turn, and single crochet across the row. Chain 1, turn, and single crochet back to the beginning. Chain 1, turn, and single crochet across the row.

When you reach your bust, start to move outward, creating the other half of the V.

Skip the first two stitches, then double crochet across the row. Double crochet back to the other side, once again skipping the last 2 stitches. Skip the first two stitches, then double crochet across the row. Double crochet back to the other side, once again skipping the last 2 stitches. Skip the first two stitches, then double crochet across the row. Double crochet back to the other side, once again skipping the last 2 stitches.

Continue until you reach the top of your shoulder.

For the sleeves:

The sleeves are going to be made to fit your arm.

Single crochet across the row. Chain 1, turn, and single crochet back to the beginning. Chain 1, turn, and single crochet across the row. Chain 1, turn, and single crochet back to the beginning. Chain 1, turn, and single crochet across the row. Chain 1, turn, and single crochet back to the beginning. Chain 1, turn, and single crochet across the row.

Sew the front pieces to the back and up the sides, leaving a hole for the arms.

Continue for the length you want your sleeves to be – this can be all the way down to your wrists, or stop at your elbows. When you are happy with the length, tie it off.

Repeat for the other side.

To finish:

Start by putting borders around all the open ends of your pieces. You want to have one end for both the cuffs, and a boarder around both the bottom and the neckline of your piece. You can do this with the same color or alternating colors – whichever you prefer.

Next, you are going to sew the arms to the body, and snip off any of the loose ends. Add any ties you would like to have on the body of the piece, and tie the ends to keep them from unraveling. Make sure all is secure, and you are done!

Conclusion

There you have it, everything you need to make a collection of warm and cozy winter wear for yourself, your friends, and all the loved ones in your life. You know this is one of the most joyful times in the year, and you want nothing more than to enjoy each and every part of it from being inside to going out and doing new things.

You know there is nothing better than when you dress up and head out into the chilly afternoon to have fun with your friends, and it's even better when you know that you look good doing it. I hope you were able to find the inspiration you need to create all kinds of warm and cozy items for your wardrobe – and as gifts for your friends and family.

There is nothing better than homemade Christmas presents, and you know you have a list of people you want to surprise with the things you can create for them. This book is going to give you the tools you need to do that, now all you need is the inspiration to make it happen.

Christmas is on the way, and you want to dive into all the festivities with a passion. You are going to find there are nothing but smiles and good times rolling when you spread the Christmas cheer with these wonderful gifts.

The meadow is full of glistening snow, and the stores are filled with all the decorations and joy of the season. You know you want to dive into all the fun of this wonderful time of year, and you can do that with nothing more than a crochet hook, your favorite yarn, and a bit of creativity and inspiration.

This book is everything you need to get started, so embrace the joy of the season with all the passion and fun you have in you, and dive into a whole new way to celebrate what this time of year has to offer. You are about to create a Christmas you are never going to forget, and you ' re going to love every second of it.

What are you waiting for? It ' s the most wonderful time of the year, and it ' s just waiting for you to dive in and take part in the joy of the season.

Good luck, and have a very happy holidays.

Crochet Ovals
6 Afghan Patterns To Use For Cozy Crochet Rugs

Introduction

You walk through your home, thinking about all the things you want to do. You want to have parties, you want to have fun for the holidays, and you want to show off what you are able to do to your friends and family. You want to create a new look that is going to be the envy of all who walk through your doors, and you want to be proud of the home you live in.

But, you also want to love the pieces you choose. You want to walk through your own home and know that you are going to love each and every piece that you choose, and you want to know without a doubt that it is going to go with the décor that you already have set in place. You don't want to settle for second best, you want to fall in love with your home and all the things you have inside.

Yet the stores don't offer the pieces that you want, and they don't give you everything you are looking for when it comes to the world of rugs. You know what you like and what you find in the stores are nice, but they aren't nearly the same thing.

So what are you going to do? Do you have to settle for second-best? Do you have to wish that you could have the rugs and décor that you dream of, but you have to go with the things that are on sale in the stores? Do you have to forget about everything you have wanted to do with your house and look like everyone else?

Thankfully, the answer is no. If you want your house to be exactly like you are dreaming, then you are going to have to decorate it yourself. You are going to have to be the one to create the pieces, and you are going to have to choose where you want them to be. It might sound intimidating, but it's not as hard as you think.

When it comes to the world of d é cor, all you need is a crochet hook and some imagination. You are going to find the inspiration with the patterns here, and you are going to see just how easy it is for you to create a variety of your own rugs. Each and every room in your house is going to look amazing, and you are going to be more than happy to show off what you can do to your friends and family.

Get ready to be the envy of all this holiday season, and fall in love with each of the pieces you create. Your rugs can be as large as you want, or you can keep them small and sweet. Mix and match until you are happy with the perfect piece, and you are going to discover just how easy it is to find the rug of your dreams.

This book is going to change the way you decorate your home, and you are going to see for yourself just how easy it is to get what you want, when you want it. The world of home d é cor is far easier to get into than you think, and you ' ll love each and every piece you find. Grab your yarn and crochet hook and settle in!

The Patterns

Basic but Beautiful Rug

You will need 4 skeins of heavy weight yarn in the colors of your choice and a size N crochet hook. T-shirt yarn and plastic yarn both work as well, and you'll still be able to use the N hook for the project.

This project is worked until you are happy with the size of the piece, so you will need as much yarn as you like to achieve that size. For a minimum, you are going to need the equivalent of 2 skeins.

Chain 10 and single crochet across the row. instead of stopping at the end of the row, you are going to continue to single crochet down and around the bottom, working until you get back to the beginning. Join with a slip stitch, forming a rounded oval.

Chain 1, turn, and single crochet back to the beginning of the row, working 1 stitch in each of the stitches along the way, once again joining with a slip stitch when you get back to the beginning. Chain 1, turn, and once again single crochet back around the edge of the piece. You are going to join with a slip stitch when you get back to the beginning once more. Chain 1, turn, and repeat back to the beginning, remembering to join with a slip stitch.

You may find that you need to add an extra stitch to the end chain to ensure that you reach properly. This is normal, and you will continue to work with this new stitch that you add along the way. You can use scrap yarn to complete this project, or you can follow the photo as a reference guide of which kind of yarn to use.

If you are using multi-colored yarn, the piece is going to stripe itself, without you having to do anything. There is no wrong way to do it, as long as you are happy with the finished rug that you have created. Tie off the previous color, join the new color with a slip stitch, and continue along the edge of the project, following the same pattern as before.

Chain 1, turn, and single crochet back around the piece back to the beginning, joining with a slip stitch when you get there. Chain 1, turn, and single crochet back to the other side, joining with a slip stitch. Chain 1, turn, and single crochet back to the beginning, joining with a slip stitch when you get to the other side. Chain 1, turn, and single crochet back to the beginning, once again joining with a slip stitch.

Chain 1, turn, and single crochet back around the piece back to the beginning, joining with a slip stitch when you get there. Chain 1, turn, and single crochet back to the other side, joining with a slip stitch. Chain 1, turn, and single crochet back to the beginning, joining with a slip stitch when you get to the other side. Chain 1, turn, and single crochet back to the beginning, once again joining with a slip stitch.

Chain 1, turn, and single crochet back around the piece back to the beginning, joining with a slip stitch when you get there. Chain 1, turn, and single crochet back to the other side, joining with a slip stitch. Chain 1, turn, and single crochet back to the beginning, joining with a slip stitch when you get to the other side. Chain 1, turn, and single crochet back to the beginning, once again joining with a slip stitch.

Continue with this until you are happy with the size of the piece, once again remembering to change colors according to the photo or your own preference.

Tie off, and make sure all the ends are secure, and your rug is done!

If you are going to be using your rug on a hard surface, consider placing rug tabs at the bottom to ensure there is no sliding when you step on the rug. These can be purchased at most craft supply stores.

Rainbow Rug

Photo made by: punktoad

You will need heavy weight yarn in the colors of your choice and a size N crochet hook. T-shirt yarn and plastic yarn both work as well, and you'll still be able to use the N hook for the project.

This project is worked until you are happy with the size of the piece, so you will need as much yarn as you like to achieve that size. For a minimum, you are going to need the equivalent of 2 skeins.

Starting with the color of your choice, you are going to chain 5 and join with a slip stitch to form a ring. Single crochet in the center of this ring 12 times, and join with a slip stitch to the beginning.

Chain 1, turn, and single crochet back to the beginning of the row, working 1 stitch in each of the stitches along the way, once again joining with a slip stitch when you get back to the beginning. Chain 1, turn, and once again single crochet back around the edge of the piece. You are going to join with a slip stitch when you get back to the beginning once more. Chain 1, turn, and repeat back to the beginning, remembering to join with a slip stitch.

You may find that you need to add an extra stitch to the end chain to ensure that you reach properly. This is normal, and you will continue to work with this new stitch that you add along the way. You can use scrap yarn to complete this project, or you can follow the photo as a reference guide of which kind of yarn to use.

If you are going to be using the photo for reference, you are going to change colors every 10 to 15 rows, or as often as you prefer. There is no wrong way to do it, as long as you are happy with the finished rug that you have created. Tie off the previous color, join the new color with a slip stitch, and continue along the edge of the project, following the same pattern as before.

Chain 1, turn, and single crochet back around the piece back to the beginning, joining with a slip stitch when you get there. Chain 1, turn, and single crochet back to the other side, joining with a slip stitch. Chain 1, turn, and single crochet back to the beginning, joining with a slip stitch when you get to the other side. Chain 1, turn, and single crochet back to the beginning, once again joining with a slip stitch.

Chain 1, turn, and single crochet back around the piece back to the beginning, joining with a slip stitch when you get there. Chain 1, turn, and single crochet back to the other side, joining with a slip stitch. Chain 1, turn, and single crochet back to the beginning, joining with a slip stitch when you get to the other side. Chain 1, turn, and single crochet back to the beginning, once again joining with a slip stitch.

Chain 1, turn, and single crochet back around the piece back to the beginning, joining with a slip stitch when you get there. Chain 1, turn, and single crochet back to the other side, joining with a slip stitch. Chain 1, turn, and single crochet back to the beginning, joining with a slip stitch when you get to the other side. Chain 1, turn, and single crochet back to the beginning, once again joining with a slip stitch.

Continue with this until you are happy with the size of the piece, once again remembering to change colors according to the photo or your own preference.

Tie off, and make sure all the ends are secure, and your rug is done!

If you are going to be using your rug on a hard surface, consider placing rug tabs at the bottom to ensure there is no sliding when you step on the rug. These can be purchased at most craft supply stores.

Perfect for Fall Rug

Photo made by: storebukkebruse

You will need heavy weight yarn in the colors of your choice and a size N crochet hook. T-shirt yarn and plastic yarn both work as well, and you'll still be able to use the N hook for the project.

This project is worked until you are happy with the size of the piece, so you will need as much yarn as you like to achieve that size. For a minimum, you are going to need the equivalent of 2 skeins.

Starting with the color of your choice, you are going to chain 5 and join with a slip stitch to form a ring. Single crochet in the center of this ring 12 times, and join with a slip stitch to the beginning.

Chain 1, turn, and single crochet back to the beginning of the row, working 1 stitch in each of the stitches along the way, once again joining with a slip stitch when you get back to the beginning. Chain 1, turn, and once again single crochet back around the edge of the piece. You are going to join with a slip stitch when you get back to the beginning once more. Chain 1, turn, and repeat back to the beginning, remembering to join with a slip stitch.

You may find that you need to add an extra stitch to the end chain to ensure that you reach properly. This is normal, and you will continue to work with this new stitch that you add along the way. You can use scrap yarn to complete this project, or you can follow the photo as a reference guide of which kind of yarn to use.

If you are going to be using the photo for reference, you are going to change colors after the first 25 rows, then again after the 50th row, then again after the 75th, or as often as you prefer. There is no wrong way to do it, as long as you are happy with the finished rug that you have created. Tie off the previous color, join the new color with a slip stitch, and continue along the edge of the project, following the same pattern as before.

Chain 1, turn, and single crochet back around the piece back to the beginning, joining with a slip stitch when you get there. Chain 1, turn, and single crochet back to the other side, joining with a slip stitch. Chain 1, turn, and single crochet back to the beginning, joining with a slip stitch when you get to the other side. Chain 1, turn, and single crochet back to the beginning, once again joining with a slip stitch.

Chain 1, turn, and single crochet back around the piece back to the beginning, joining with a slip stitch when you get there. Chain 1, turn, and single crochet back to the other side, joining with a slip stitch. Chain 1, turn, and single crochet back to the beginning, joining with a slip stitch when you get to the other side. Chain 1, turn, and single crochet back to the beginning, once again joining with a slip stitch.

Chain 1, turn, and single crochet back around the piece back to the beginning, joining with a slip stitch when you get there. Chain 1, turn, and single crochet back to the other side, joining with a slip stitch. Chain 1, turn, and single crochet back to the beginning, joining with a slip stitch when you get to the other side. Chain 1, turn, and single crochet back to the beginning, once again joining with a slip stitch.

Continue with this until you are happy with the size of the piece, once again remembering to change colors according to the photo or your own preference.

Tie off, and make sure all the ends are secure, and your rug is done!

If you are going to be using your rug on a hard surface, consider placing rug tabs at the bottom to ensure there is no sliding when you step on the rug. These can be purchased at most craft supply stores.

Rags to Riches Rug

Photo made by: Rick&Brenda Beerhorst

You will need heavy weight yarn in the colors of your choice and a size N crochet hook. T-shirt yarn and plastic yarn both work as well, and you'll still be able to use the N hook for the project.

This project is worked until you are happy with the size of the piece, so you will need as much yarn as you like to achieve that size. For a minimum, you are going to need the equivalent of 2 skeins.

Starting with the color of your choice, you are going to chain 5 and join with a slip stitch to form a ring. Single crochet in the center of this ring 12 times, and join with a slip stitch to the beginning.

Chain 1, turn, and single crochet back to the beginning of the row, working 1 stitch in each of the stitches along the way, once again joining with a slip stitch when you get back to the beginning. Chain 1, turn, and once again single crochet back around the edge of the piece. You are going to join with a slip stitch when you get back to the beginning once more. Chain 1, turn, and repeat back to the beginning, remembering to join with a slip stitch.

You may find that you need to add an extra stitch to the end chain to ensure that you reach properly. This is normal, and you will continue to work with this new stitch that you add along the way. You can use scrap yarn to complete this project, or you can follow the photo as a reference guide of which kind of yarn to use.

If you are going to be using the photo for reference, you are going to change colors every 10 to 15 rows, or as often as you prefer. There is no wrong way to do it, as long as you are happy with the finished rug that you have created. Tie off the previous color, join the new color with a slip stitch, and continue along the edge of the project, following the same pattern as before.

Chain 1, turn, and single crochet back around the piece back to the beginning, joining with a slip stitch when you get there. Chain 1, turn, and single crochet back to the other side, joining with a slip stitch. Chain 1, turn, and single crochet back to the beginning, joining with a slip stitch when you get to the other side. Chain 1, turn, and single crochet back to the beginning, once again joining with a slip stitch.

Chain 1, turn, and single crochet back around the piece back to the beginning, joining with a slip stitch when you get there. Chain 1, turn, and single crochet back to the other side, joining with a slip stitch. Chain 1, turn, and single crochet back to the beginning, joining with a slip stitch when you get to the other side. Chain 1, turn, and single crochet back to the beginning, once again joining with a slip stitch.

Chain 1, turn, and single crochet back around the piece back to the beginning, joining with a slip stitch when you get there. Chain 1, turn, and single crochet back to the other side, joining with a slip stitch. Chain 1, turn, and single crochet back to the beginning, joining with a slip stitch when you get to the other side. Chain 1, turn, and single crochet back to the beginning, once again joining with a slip stitch.

Continue with this until you are happy with the size of the piece, once again remembering to change colors according to the photo or your own preference.

Tie off, and make sure all the ends are secure, and your rug is done!

If you are going to be using your rug on a hard surface, consider placing rug tabs at the bottom to ensure there is no sliding when you step on the rug. These can be purchased at most craft supply stores.

Seasonal Sensation Rug

Photo made by: Rick&Brenda Beerhorst

You will need heavy weight yarn in the colors of your choice and a size N crochet hook. T-shirt yarn and plastic yarn both work as well, and you'll still be able to use the N hook for the project.

This project is worked until you are happy with the size of the piece, so you will need as much yarn as you like to achieve that size. For a minimum, you are going to need the equivalent of 2 skeins.

Starting with the color of your choice, you are going to chain 5 and join with a slip stitch to form a ring. Single crochet in the center of this ring 12 times, and join with a slip stitch to the beginning.

Chain 1, turn, and single crochet back to the beginning of the row, working 1 stitch in each of the stitches along the way, once again joining with a slip stitch when you get back to the beginning. Chain 1, turn, and once again single crochet back around the edge of the piece. You are going to join with a slip stitch when you get back to the beginning once more. Chain 1, turn, and repeat back to the beginning, remembering to join with a slip stitch.

You may find that you need to add an extra stitch to the end chain to ensure that you reach properly. This is normal, and you will continue to work with this new stitch that you add along the way. You can use scrap yarn to complete this project, or you can follow the photo as a reference guide of which kind of yarn to use.

If you are going to be using the photo for reference, you are going to change colors every other row, or as often as you prefer. There is no wrong way to do it, as long as you are happy with the finished rug that you have created. Tie off the previous color, join the new color with a slip stitch, and continue along the edge of the project, following the same pattern as before.

Chain 1, turn, and single crochet back around the piece back to the beginning, joining with a slip stitch when you get there. Chain 1, turn, and single crochet back to the other side, joining with a slip stitch. Chain 1, turn, and single crochet back to the beginning, joining with a slip stitch when you get to the other side. Chain 1, turn, and single crochet back to the beginning, once again joining with a slip stitch.

Chain 1, turn, and single crochet back around the piece back to the beginning, joining with a slip stitch when you get there. Chain 1, turn, and single crochet back to the other side, joining with a slip stitch. Chain 1, turn, and single crochet back to the beginning, joining with a slip stitch when you get to the other side. Chain 1, turn, and single crochet back to the beginning, once again joining with a slip stitch.

Chain 1, turn, and single crochet back around the piece back to the beginning, joining with a slip stitch when you get there. Chain 1, turn, and single crochet back to the other side, joining with a slip stitch. Chain 1, turn, and single crochet back to the beginning, joining with a slip stitch when you get to the other side. Chain 1, turn, and single crochet back to the beginning, once again joining with a slip stitch.

Continue with this until you are happy with the size of the piece, once again remembering to change colors according to the photo or your own preference.

Tie off, and make sure all the ends are secure, and your rug is done!

If you are going to be using your rug on a hard surface, consider placing rug tabs at the bottom to ensure there is no sliding when you step on the rug. These can be purchased at most craft supply stores.

The Hodge Podge Edition

Photo made by: Max Barners

You will need heavy weight yarn in the colors of your choice and a size N crochet hook. T-shirt yarn and plastic yarn both work as well, and you'll still be able to use the N hook for the project.

This project is worked until you are happy with the size of the piece, so you will need as much yarn as you like to achieve that size. For a minimum, you are going to need the equivalent of 2 skeins.

Starting with the color of your choice, you are going to chain 5 and join with a slip stitch to form a ring. Single crochet in the center of this ring 12 times, and join with a slip stitch to the beginning.

Chain 1, turn, and single crochet back to the beginning of the row, working 1 stitch in each of the stitches along the way, once again joining with a slip stitch when you get back to the beginning. Chain 1, turn, and once again single crochet back around the edge of the piece. You are going to join with a slip stitch when you get back to the beginning once more. Chain 1, turn, and repeat back to the beginning, remembering to join with a slip stitch.

You may find that you need to add an extra stitch to the end chain to ensure that you reach properly. This is normal, and you will continue to work with this new stitch that you add along the way. You can use scrap yarn to complete this project, or you can follow the photo as a reference guide of which kind of yarn to use.

If you are using multi-colored yarn, the piece is going to stripe itself, without you having to do anything. There is no wrong way to do it, as long as you are happy with the finished rug that you have created. Tie off the previous color, join the new color with a slip stitch, and continue along the edge of the project, following the same pattern as before.

Chain 1, turn, and single crochet back around the piece back to the beginning, joining with a slip stitch when you get there. Chain 1, turn, and single crochet back to the other side, joining with a slip stitch. Chain 1, turn, and single crochet back to the beginning, joining with a slip stitch when you get to the other side. Chain 1, turn, and single crochet back to the beginning, once again joining with a slip stitch.

Chain 1, turn, and single crochet back around the piece back to the beginning, joining with a slip stitch when you get there. Chain 1, turn, and single crochet back to the other side, joining with a slip stitch.

Chain 1, turn, and single crochet back to the beginning, joining with a slip stitch when you get to the other side. Chain 1, turn, and single crochet back to the beginning, once again joining with a slip stitch.

Chain 1, turn, and single crochet back around the piece back to the beginning, joining with a slip stitch when you get there. Chain 1, turn, and single crochet back to the other side, joining with a slip stitch. Chain 1, turn, and single crochet back to the beginning, joining with a slip stitch when you get to the other side. Chain 1, turn, and single crochet back to the beginning, once again joining with a slip stitch.

Continue with this until you are happy with the size of the piece, once again remembering to change colors according to the photo or your own preference.

Tie off, and make sure all the ends are secure, and your rug is done!

If you are going to be using your rug on a hard surface, consider placing rug tabs at the bottom to ensure there is no sliding when you step on the rug. These can be purchased at most craft supply stores.

Conclusion

There you have it, everything you need to know to make your own afghan rugs, and the patterns to inspire you to create something wonderful with them to decorate every room in your house.

When it comes to home décor, the only way to get what you truly want is to make it yourself. Sure, you can find things in the store that you like. You can look at patterns and designs that you think are pretty, and you can find things that go with the rest of your house, but when you are looking for something that is created for your house – something that is going to make your house look wonderful and bring out just what you wanted in the room, you are going to have to do it yourself.

I hope this book was able to fill you with the inspiration you need to create a variety of beautiful rugs for your home, and that you are thrilled with each and every rug you have. There is no end to the ways you can fall in love with the rugs you wish to create, and you are going to find that each one is full of personality and charm.

Turn your home into the palace you have been dreaming of, and enjoy a variety of rugs that only you can create. Your friends and family will be amazed with the results, and you are going to find that there really is no end to the ways you can spice up the look of your home with just a simple piece.

So what are you waiting for? The holidays are on their way, and with them come all the family and friends. Hosting has never felt better than when you are able to take your home décor up to the next level, and the fun you are going to have as you show off each room to your friends and family is going to make all the hard work worth it.

Get out to the store, find your favorite yarn and crochet hook, and settle in. You are going to fall in love with the results, and you are going to be amazed at just how easy it is for you to create d é cor for your home that lasts a lifetime.

You ' ll be making memories as much as you are making the perfect decoration piece, and you ' ll see for yourself just how good it is to create what you want, when you want. There really is no end to the ways you can show off your style, all you have to do is imagine, take inspiration, and showcase your creativity. It all comes down to what you want to do with your look, and what you are able to make with your hook.

Getting that perfect room has never been so easy.

You ' ve got the perfect look waiting for you – you just have to create it.

Good luck.

Crochet Dream Catchers:
10 Mystic Dream Catchers To Protect Your Sleep

Introduction

You have dreams, hopes, and ambitions, and you want to follow all of them. You sleep well, you wake up, and you remember some of the dreams that you had, but other times, your dreams just feel like a distant memory.

There are times your dreams aren't so sweet, and you fear going back to sleep lest you somehow end up back inside one of them. You spend a night worried about this, and you wake up feeling tired and groggy the next day. It doesn't really matter what you do, when you fall asleep, it is little more than a gamble.

You want something that is going to help you sleep well. Something that is going to capture your imagination, fill you with motivation, and provide that sweet night you have been yearning for. No, you don't want medication and you certainly don't want to take any kind of pill – you want something that has been around longer than either of those.

You want a dreamcatcher.

But, how are you going to get one?

Sure, you can get online and order one. You can go to the store and buy one, but they aren't going to be personal. They aren't going to give you the end result you are looking for. To do that, you are going to have to do it yourself.

You are going to have to make one.

But, you ask – is that hard?

Is there a way you can do it without too much trouble?

How do you get them to fit inside those rings?

With all these questions in your head, it is easy to feel overwhelmed. But, this book is going to change all that, and it is going to provide you with the simple directions you need to create your very own dreamcatchers. This book is everything you have been searching for, and it is going to help you chase your dreams.

So what are you waiting for? All you need are a few tools to get the job done – and with this book, you've got them handed to you right here, and right now.

Let's get started – you have some dreaming to do.

The Dream Catchers

Mystic Mountain Dreamcatcher

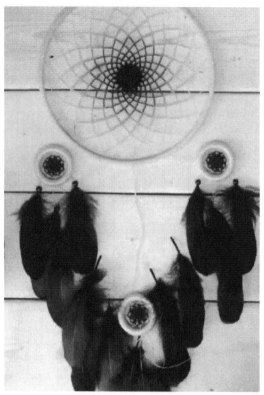

You will need thread weight yarn in the colors of your choice and a size G crochet hook.

You will also need a needle and thread, a hoop in the size of your choice, and any decorations you wish to add to the finished catcher.

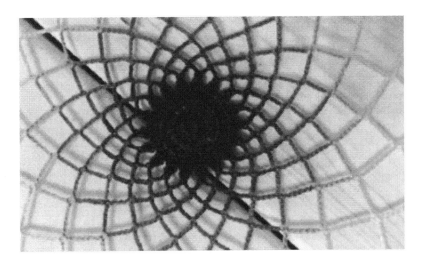

Chain 5 and join with a slip stitch to form a ring. Single crochet in the center of this ring 12 times, and join with a slip stitch. Chain 1, turn, and single crochet back to the other side, using 1 stitch in each stitch. Join with a slip stitch, chain 1, turn, and go back the other way, following the same pattern.

Continue to do this until the center measures 2 inches across.

For the next row, you are going to chain 5 and skip the next stitch and join with a slip stitch in the next stitch. Chain 5 and skip the next stitch then join with a slip stitch in the next stitch. Chain 5 and skip the next stitch then join with a slip stitch in the next stitch. Continue around.

Chain 5 and join with a slip stitch in the center of the chain space. Chain 5 once more and join with a slip stitch in the center of the next chain space. Continue around.

Repeat the last row until the piece is nearly as big as the hoop you are going to use. Tie off and set aside.

Repeat this sequence twice more for the two smaller hoops –
set both aside.

To assemble:

Take your piece now and stretch it slightly to fit in the ring. Remember that you are going to make it slightly too small to fit the ring, so you have a nice, tight stretch when it is time to put it in.

Use your needle and thread to sew around the outside of the piece you have crocheted, wrapping it around the outside of the ring, and through the piece once more. Continue with even stitches all the way around the piece until you are happy with the center.

Tie off.

Add any additional ornaments you like to the centerpiece as well as the outside bottom of the ring. Attach a hook or a loop at the top to hang the piece, and you are done!

King of the Sea Dreamcatcher

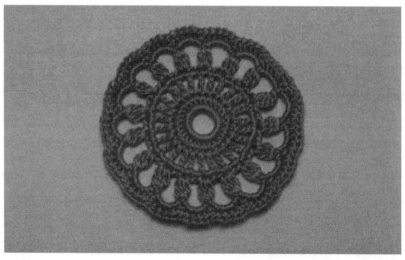

You will need thread weight yarn in the colors of your choice and a size G crochet hook.

You will also need a needle and thread, a hoop in the size of your choice, and any decorations you wish to add to the finished catcher.

Chain 10 and join with a slip stitch. Single crochet back around to the other side. Chain 1, turn, and single crochet back to the beginning.

Join with a slip stitch. Chain 1, turn, and single crochet back to the other side. Continue for a total of 5 rows.

For the next row, you are going to chain 5 and skip the next stitch and join with a slip stitch in the next stitch. Chain 5 and skip the next stitch then join with a slip stitch in the next stitch. Chain 5 and skip the next stitch then join with a slip stitch in the next stitch. Continue around.

You are now going to go back to single crochet for the next 3 rows, joining the tops of the humps you have created from the previous row. You may have to chain a few extra stitches between the humps to ensure that you get the right shape to the piece, so work with the piece until you are happy with the shape.

For the next row, you are going to chain 8 and skip the next 4 stitches, then join with a slip stitch in the next stitch. For the next row, you are going to chain 8 and skip the next 4 stitches, then join with a slip stitch in the next stitch. For the next row, you are going to chain 8 and skip the next 4 stitches, then join with a slip stitch in the next stitch. For the next row, you are going to chain 8 and skip the next 4 stitches, then join with a slip stitch in the next stitch.

Repeat the last row until the piece is nearly as big as the hoop you are going to use.

For the next row, you are going to single crochet around the boarder of your piece 2 times. Again, you want this to still be smaller than the hoop of your choice, so don ' t make this border too thick.

When you are happy with the size, tie it off and set aside.

To assemble:

Take your piece now and stretch it slightly to fit in the ring. Remember that you are going to make it slightly too small to fit the ring, so you have a nice, tight stretch when it is time to put it in.

Use your needle and thread to sew around the outside of the piece you have crocheted, wrapping it around the outside of the ring, and through the piece once more. Continue with even stitches all the way around the piece until you are happy with the center.

Tie off.

Add any additional ornaments you like to the centerpiece as well as the outside bottom of the ring. Attach a hook or a loop at the top to hang the piece, and you are done!

Perfect for Fall Dreamcatcher

You will need thread weight yarn in the colors of your choice and a size G crochet hook.

You will also need a needle and thread, a hoop in the size of your choice, and any decorations you wish to add to the finished catcher.

Chain 5 and join with a slip stitch to form a ring. Single crochet in the center of this ring 12 times, and join with a slip stitch. Chain 1, turn, and single crochet back to the other side, using 1 stitch in each stitch. Join with a slip stitch, chain 1, turn, and go back the other way, following the same pattern.

Continue to do this until the center measures 2 inches across.

For the next row, you are going to chain 5 and skip the next stitch and join with a slip stitch in the next stitch. Chain 5 and skip the next stitch then join with a slip stitch in the next stitch. Chain 5 and skip the next stitch then join with a slip stitch in the next stitch. Continue around.

Chain 5 and join with a slip stitch in the center of the chain space. Chain 5 once more and join with a slip stitch in the center of the next chain space. Continue around.

Repeat the last row until the piece is nearly as big as the hoop you are going to use. Tie off and set aside.

Remember to attach beads to the ends as you stitch this to the hoop of your choice.

To assemble:

Take your piece now and stretch it slightly to fit in the ring. Remember that you are going to make it slightly too small to fit the ring, so you have a nice, tight stretch when it is time to put it in.

Use your needle and thread to sew around the outside of the piece you have crocheted, wrapping it around the outside of the ring, and through the piece once more. Continue with even stitches all the way around the piece until you are happy with the center.

Tie off.

Add any additional ornaments you like to the centerpiece as well as the outside bottom of the ring. Attach a hook or a loop at the top to hang the piece, and you are done!

Spring Center Dreamcatcher

You will need thread weight yarn in the colors of your choice and a size G crochet hook.

You will also need a needle and thread, a hoop in the size of your choice, and any decorations you wish to add to the finished catcher.

Chain 5 and join with a slip stitch to form a ring. Single crochet in the center of this ring 12 times, and join with a slip stitch. Chain 1, turn, and single crochet back to the other side, using 1 stitch in each stitch. Join with a slip stitch, chain 1, turn, and go back the other way, following the same pattern.

Continue to do this until the center measures 2 inches across.

Tie off this color and join with the next color.

For the next row, you are going to chain 5 and skip the next stitch and join with a slip stitch in the next stitch. Chain 5 and skip the next stitch then join with a slip stitch in the next stitch. Chain 5 and skip the next stitch then join with a slip stitch in the next stitch. Continue around.

Chain 5 and join with a slip stitch in the center of the chain space. Chain 5 once more and join with a slip stitch in the center of the next chain space. Continue around.

Repeat the last row until the piece is nearly as big as the hoop you are going to use. Tie off and set aside.

Remember to repeat this two more times for the other hoops. You are going to follow the same sequence throughout, just alter the piece to fit the hoop you are currently making it for.

To assemble:

Take your piece now and stretch it slightly to fit in the ring. Remember that you are going to make it slightly too small to fit the ring, so you have a nice, tight stretch when it is time to put it in.

Use your needle and thread to sew around the outside of the piece you have crocheted, wrapping it around the outside of the ring, and through the piece once more. Continue with even stitches all the way around the piece until you are happy with the center.

Tie off.

Add any additional ornaments you like to the centerpiece as well as the outside bottom of the ring. Attach a hook or a loop at the top to hang the piece, and you are done!

Pretty in Pink Dreamcatcher

You will need thread weight yarn in the colors of your choice and a size G crochet hook.

You will also need a needle and thread, a hoop in the size of your choice, and any decorations you wish to add to the finished catcher.

Chain 5 and join with a slip stitch to form a ring. Single crochet in the center of this ring 12 times, and join with a slip stitch. Chain 1, turn, and single crochet back to the other side, using 1 stitch in each stitch. Join with a slip stitch, chain 1, turn, and go back the other way, following the same pattern.

Continue to do this until the center measures 2 inches across.

Change colors and join with the next color (for the larger hoop only.)

For the next row, you are going to chain 5 and skip the next stitch and join with a slip stitch in the next stitch. Chain 5 and skip the next stitch then join with a slip stitch in the next stitch. Chain 5 and skip the next stitch then join with a slip stitch in the next stitch. Continue around.

Chain 5 and join with a slip stitch in the center of the chain space. Chain 5 once more and join with a slip stitch in the center of the next chain space. Continue around.

Repeat the last row until the piece is nearly as big as the hoop you are going to use. Tie off and set aside.

You are going to now go back and repeat this sequence for the smaller three hoops. Remember that you are not going to change colors for those pieces.

To assemble:

Take your piece now and stretch it slightly to fit in the ring. Remember that you are going to make it slightly too small to fit the ring, so you have a nice, tight stretch when it is time to put it in.

Use your needle and thread to sew around the outside of the piece you have crocheted, wrapping it around the outside of the ring, and through the piece once more. Continue with even stitches all the way around the piece until you are happy with the center.

Tie off.

Add any additional ornaments you like to the centerpiece as well as the outside bottom of the ring. Attach a hook or a loop at the top to hang the piece, and you are done!

Delicate Lace Dreamcatcher

You will need thread weight yarn in the colors of your choice and a size G crochet hook.

You will also need a needle and thread, a hoop in the size of your choice, and any decorations you wish to add to the finished catcher.

Chain 10 and join with a slip stitch. Single crochet back around to the other side. Chain 1, turn, and single crochet back to the beginning. Join with a slip stitch. Chain 1, turn, and single crochet back to the other side. Continue for a total of 5 rows.

For the next row, you are going to chain 5 and skip the next stitch and join with a slip stitch in the next stitch. Chain 5 and skip the next stitch then join with a slip stitch in the next stitch. Chain 5 and skip the next stitch then join with a slip stitch in the next stitch. Continue around.

You are now going to go back to single crochet for the next 7-8 rows, joining the tops of the humps you have created from the previous row. You may have to chain a few extra stitches between the humps to ensure that you get the right shape to the piece, so work with the piece until you are happy with the shape.

How thick you make this second piece is going to depend on the overall size of the hoop you are using, as well as the piece itself. Don't be afraid to adjust within the piece as you are working to ensure that you get the right shape and the right thickness – the good thing about these dreamcatchers is that you are able to adjust them to fit your needs as you work, instead of having to go with the black and white directions to get them the proper shape.

Make this thicker or even thinner if you are going to be using a smaller hoop, as long as you are happy with the end result, you are doing it the right way.

For the next row, you are going to chain 5 and skip the next stitch and join with a slip stitch in the next stitch. Chain 5 and skip the next stitch then join with a slip stitch in the next stitch. Chain 5 and skip the next stitch then join with a slip stitch in the next stitch. Continue around.

Chain 5 and join with a slip stitch in the center of the chain space. Chain 5 once more and join with a slip stitch in the center of the next chain space. Continue around.

Repeat the last row until the piece is nearly as big as the hoop you are going to use. Tie off and set aside.

To assemble:

Take your piece now and stretch it slightly to fit in the ring. Remember that you are going to make it slightly too small to fit the ring, so you have a nice, tight stretch when it is time to put it in.

Use your needle and thread to sew around the outside of the piece you have crocheted, wrapping it around the outside of the ring, and through the piece once more. Continue with even stitches all the way around the piece until you are happy with the center.

Tie off.

Add any additional ornaments you like to the centerpiece as well as the outside bottom of the ring. Attach a hook or a loop at the top to hang the piece, and you are done!

Catching the Wind Dreamcatcher

Photo made by: flyone1106

You will need thread weight yarn in the colors of your choice and a size G crochet hook.

You will also need a needle and thread, a hoop in the size of your choice, and any decorations you wish to add to the finished catcher.

Chain 5 and join with a slip stitch to form a ring. Single crochet in the center of this ring 12 times, and join with a slip stitch. Chain 1, turn, and single crochet back to the other side, using 1 stitch in each stitch. Join with a slip stitch, chain 1, turn, and go back the other way, following the same pattern.

Depending on the size of your piece, you can make the center as thick as you want, or leave it on the small side. Use the photo as a reference for the size of your piece.

For the next row, you are going to chain 5 and skip the next stitch and join with a slip stitch in the next stitch. Chain 5 and skip the next stitch then join with a slip stitch in the next stitch. Chain 5 and skip the next stitch then join with a slip stitch in the next stitch. Continue around.

Chain 5 and join with a slip stitch in the center of the chain space. Chain 5 once more and join with a slip stitch in the center of the next chain space. Continue around.

Repeat the last row until the piece is nearly as big as the hoop you are going to use. Tie off and set aside.

To assemble:

Take your piece now and stretch it slightly to fit in the ring. Remember that you are going to make it slightly too small to fit the ring, so you have a nice, tight stretch when it is time to put it in.

Use your needle and thread to sew around the outside of the piece you have crocheted, wrapping it around the outside of the ring, and through the piece once more. Continue with even stitches all the way around the piece until you are happy with the center.

Tie off.

Add any additional ornaments you like to the centerpiece as well as the outside bottom of the ring. Attach a hook or a loop at the top to hang the piece, and you are done!

Mini Beaded Dreamcatcher

Photo made by: amylovesyah

You will need thread weight yarn in the colors of your choice and a size G crochet hook.

You will also need a needle and thread, a hoop in the size of your choice, and any decorations you wish to add to the finished catcher.

Chain 5 and join with a slip stitch to form a ring. Single crochet in the center of this ring 12 times, and join with a slip stitch. Chain 1, turn, and single crochet back to the other side, using 1 stitch in each stitch. Join with a slip stitch, chain 1, turn, and go back the other way, following the same pattern.

Depending on the size of your piece, you can make the center as thick as you want, or leave it on the small side. Use the photo as a reference for the size of your piece.

For the next row, you are going to chain 5 and skip the next stitch and join with a slip stitch in the next stitch. Chain 5 and skip the next stitch then join with a slip stitch in the next stitch. Chain 5 and skip the next stitch then join with a slip stitch in the next stitch. Continue around.

Chain 5 and join with a slip stitch in the center of the chain space. Chain 5 once more and join with a slip stitch in the center of the next chain space. Continue around.

Repeat the last row until the piece is nearly as big as the hoop you are going to use. Tie off and set aside.

Add the beads to the piece after you have it sewn in place.

To assemble:

Take your piece now and stretch it slightly to fit in the ring. Remember that you are going to make it slightly too small to fit the ring, so you have a nice, tight stretch when it is time to put it in.

Use your needle and thread to sew around the outside of the piece you have crocheted, wrapping it around the outside of the ring, and through the piece once more. Continue with even stitches all the way around the piece until you are happy with the center.

Tie off.

Add any additional ornaments you like to the centerpiece as well as the outside bottom of the ring. Attach a hook or a loop at the top to hang the piece, and you are done!

Triple Crown Dreamcatcher

Photo made by: mikeporterinmd

You will need thread weight yarn in the colors of your choice and a size G crochet hook.

You will also need a needle and thread, a hoop in the size of your choice, and any decorations you wish to add to the finished catcher.

Chain 5 and join with a slip stitch to form a ring. Single crochet in the center of this ring 12 times, and join with a slip stitch. Chain 1, turn, and single crochet back to the other side, using 1 stitch in each stitch. Join with a slip stitch, chain 1, turn, and go back the other way, following the same pattern.

Depending on the size of your piece, you can make the center as thick as you want, or leave it on the small side. Use the photo as a reference for the size of your piece.

For the next row, you are going to chain 5 and skip the next stitch and join with a slip stitch in the next stitch. Chain 5 and skip the next stitch then join with a slip stitch in the next stitch. Chain 5 and skip the next stitch then join with a slip stitch in the next stitch. Continue around.

Chain 5 and join with a slip stitch in the center of the chain space. Chain 5 once more and join with a slip stitch in the center of the next chain space. Continue around.

Repeat the last row until the piece is nearly as big as the hoop you are going to use. Tie off and set aside.

Add the beads to the main part of the piece after you have it sewn securely into place.

To assemble:

Take your piece now and stretch it slightly to fit in the ring. Remember that you are going to make it slightly too small to fit the ring, so you have a nice, tight stretch when it is time to put it in.

Use your needle and thread to sew around the outside of the piece you have crocheted, wrapping it around the outside of the ring, and through the piece once more. Continue with even stitches all the way around the piece until you are happy with the center.

Tie off.

Add any additional ornaments you like to the centerpiece as well as the outside bottom of the ring. Attach a hook or a loop at the top to hang the piece, and you are done!

Now that you have your dreamcatchers, it's time to decorate! Of course, you can follow each of the images and decorate them with real feathers, or you can crochet your own. For this final project, we are going to look at how you can crochet your own feathers.

Crochet Feathers

Photo made by: Regina Rioux

You will need 1 ball of cotton yarn in the color of your choice and a size G crochet hook.

Decide how long you want your feather to be, and chain a length that is equal to this measurement. Single crochet back to the beginning. Next, take your hook and slip stitch to the base of where you want the feather to start fanning out.

Chain 10 and join with a slip stitch to the same stitch. Chain 10 and repeat on the other side. Now, move to the next stitch. Chain 10, and join with a slip stitch in the first stitch. Chain 10 and repeat on the other side. Chain 10 and join with a slip stitch to the same stitch. Chain 10 and repeat on the other side. Now, move to the next stitch. Chain 10, and join with a slip stitch in the first stitch. Chain 10 and repeat on the other side.

Chain 10 and join with a slip stitch to the same stitch. Chain 10 and repeat on the other side. Now, move to the next stitch. Chain 10, and join with a slip stitch in the first stitch. Chain 10 and repeat on the other side. Chain 10 and join with a slip stitch to the same stitch. Chain 10 and repeat on the other side. Now, move to the next stitch. Chain 10, and join with a slip stitch in the first stitch. Chain 10 and repeat on the other side.

Use the photo as reference, and as you get closer to the end, begin to chain fewer stitches to taper the end of the feather. Leave a point at the very end, and tie off the yarn.

That's it! Make as many of these as you like and your feathers are done!

Conclusion

There you have it, everything you need to know to make your own collection of dreamcatchers. It's no secret that these pieces are some of the most enchanting things you can use to decorate your home, and when you know how to make them yourself, you are giving yourself everything you need to decorate your house the right way.

I hope you make each and every one of the pieces you find in this book, and that you are able to take each of these and throw in your own creativity. There is no end to the ways you can show off your style, and with dreamcatchers, you're going to be sleeping well all night – every night.

Good luck, and sweet dreams.

Fall Crochet Patterns
20 Cozy Fall Crochet Projects For You And Your Home

Introduction

It's getting on to be that time of the year, and you are ready to celebrate. From holidays and getting together with friends and family to enjoying all kinds of good times with those you love, you are ready for the days to come.

You know amid all the festivities you want to decorate. You want to embrace your style, and you want to enjoy all this season has to offer. Of course, in order to do that, you are going to have to express your creative side in a whole new way – and this book is going to show you how.

Discover all kinds of new ways to create a style that is uniquely yours. From all the things you can make to decorate your house to the things you can create to show off your style, you are going to find it here.

This book is going to show you how to create anything and everything you like, and you are going to discover that there really is no way you can go wrong. This book is everything you have been looking for and then some, and you are going to get just what you are looking for.

Unleash your inner creativity, and you are going to get the projects you have been dreaming of. You know you want to, and now you can. Let's get started.

Chapter 1 – The Projects

Pumpkin Patch

Photo made by: 0Cassandra0Clevenger0

You will need 1 skein of yarn in each of the colors you wish to use and a size G crochet hook

Chain 4 and join with a slip stitch to form a ring. Single crochet in the center of this ring 10 times, and join with another slip stitch.

Chain 1, turn, and single crochet around the row. Chain 1, turn, and single crochet back around, joining with a slip stitch when you get back to the beginning. Chain 1, turn, and single crochet back to the beginning. Chain 1, turn, and single crochet back to the beginning, joining with a slip stitch.

Continue with this until you have a disc that is 8 inches across, then begin your decrease.

Chain 1, turn, and single crochet in the first 5 stitches, then skip the next stitch. Single crochet in the next 5 stitches, then skip the next stitch. Single crochet in the next 5 stitches, then skip the next stitch. Single crochet in the next 5 stitches, then skip the next stitch. Single crochet in the next 5 stitches, then skip the next stitch.

Once the pumpkin begins to form, you are going to work a few rows without decreasing, before returning to the decrease to finish the ball shape.

Stuff the pumpkins with stuffing, and when you are done, sew the bottom. Take a yarn needle and lengths of yarn, then form the shapes of the pumpkins. Tie off, and make sure all is secure.

That's it! Your pumpkins are done!

Fall Wraps

Photo made by: smittenkittenoriginals

You will need 1 skein of yarn in each of the colors you wish to use and a size J crochet hook

Chain a length that is 6 feet long.

Single crochet across the row. Chain 1, turn, and single crochet back to the beginning, in the front loop only. Chain 2, turn, and double crochet across the row. Chain 2, turn, and double crochet back to the beginning, in the front loop only. Chain 2, turn, and double crochet across the row in the front loop only. Chain 2, turn, and double crochet back to the beginning, in the front loop only.

Chain 2, turn, and double crochet across the row, in the front loop only. Chain 2, turn, and double crochet back to the beginning in the front loop only. Chain 2, turn, and double crochet back to the beginning in the front loop only. Chain 2, turn, and double crochet back to the beginning in the front loop only. Chain 2, turn, and double crochet back to the beginning in the front loop only.

Continue until you are happy with the size of the scarf, and tie off. Add fringe to the end and you are done!

Carrie the Cranberry

Photo made by: snarledskein

You will need 1 skein of yarn in each of the colors you wish to use and a size G crochet hook

Chain 4 and join with a slip stitch to form a ring. Single crochet in the center of this ring 10 times, and join with another slip stitch.

Chain 1, turn, and single crochet around the row. Chain 1, turn, and single crochet back around, joining with a slip stitch when you get back to the beginning. Chain 1, turn, and single crochet back to the beginning. Chain 1, turn, and single crochet back to the beginning, joining with a slip stitch.

Continue with this until you have a disc that is 4 inches across, then begin your decrease.

Chain 1, turn, and single crochet in the first 2 stitches, then skip the next stitch. Single crochet in the next 2 stitches, then skip the next stitch. Single crochet in the next 2 stitches, then skip the next stitch. Single crochet in the next 2 stitches, then skip the next stitch. Single crochet in the next 2 stitches, then skip the next stitch.

Once the cranberry begins to form, you are going to work a few rows without decreasing, before returning to the decrease to finish the ball shape.

Stuff the cranberry with stuffing, and when you are done, sew the bottom. Use green and smaller discs to form the leaves, then attach these with chains.

Sew on the buttons for the eyes and stitch on the remaining details, and your cranberry is done!

The Fall Bangle

Photo made by: Maria Panayiotou

You will need 1 skein of yarn in each of the colors you wish to use and a size G crochet hook

Using fun fur yarn, wrap around your bangle. Make sure that there are no spaces in between the strands. Continue to wrap until you reach the other side, then take your crochet hook and feed it through the bottom of the piece.

Make sure everything is secure, then tie off.

Not Your Mother's Scarf

Photo made by: macrak

You will need 1 skein of yarn in each of the colors you wish to use and a size J crochet hook

Choose 5 or 6 colors and take your crochet hook. Chain a length that is 4 feet long, then tie it off and set it aside. Repeat this for the other colors, making each one the same length.

Once you have all the colors, hold them together and tie knots in the chain. Tie one final knot, securing the scarf together, and you are done!

Fall Bash Beanie

Photo made by: paeonia1

You will need 1 skein of yarn in each of the colors you wish to use and a size G crochet hook

Chain 4 and join with a slip stitch to form a ring. Single crochet in the center of this ring 10 times, and join with another slip stitch.

Chain 1, turn, and single crochet around the row. Chain 1, turn, and single crochet back around, joining with a slip stitch when you get back to the beginning. Chain 1, turn, and single crochet back to the beginning. Chain 1, turn, and single crochet back to the beginning, joining with a slip stitch.

Continue with this until you have a disc fits across the top of your head, then begin your decrease.

Chain 1, turn, and single crochet in the first 5 stitches, then skip the next stitch. Single crochet in the next 5 stitches, then skip the next stitch. Single crochet in the next 5 stitches, then skip the next stitch. Single crochet in the next 5 stitches, then skip the next stitch. Single crochet in the next 5 stitches, then skip the next stitch.

Once the hat fits the shape of your head, you are going to work a few rows without decreasing, continuing until the hat is the length that you prefer.

Once the hat as reached your desired length, tie off and you are done!

The Fall Collection Washcloths

Photo made by: smittenkittenoriginals

You will need 1 skein of yarn in each of the colors you wish to use and a size G crochet hook

Chain a length that is 8 inches long.

Single crochet across the row. Chain 1, turn, and single crochet back to the beginning. Chain 1, turn, and single crochet across the row. Chain 1, turn, and single crochet back to the beginning. Chain 1, turn, and single crochet back to the beginning. Chain 1, turn, and single crochet across the row. Chain 1, turn, and single crochet back to the beginning. Chain 1, turn, and single crochet back to the beginning. Chain 1, turn, and single crochet across the row. Chain 1, turn, and single crochet back to the beginning.

Chain 1, turn, and single crochet across the row. Chain 1, turn, and single crochet back to the beginning. Chain 1, turn, and single crochet back to the beginning. Chain 1, turn, and single crochet across the row. Chain 1, turn, and single crochet back to the beginning. Chain 1, turn, and single crochet back to the beginning. Chain 1, turn, and single crochet across the row. Chain 1, turn, and single crochet back to the beginning.

Continue until you have a square, then tie off. Single crochet around the border, and you are done!

Repeat for the other washcloths, and you are done!

Maroon Madness

Photo made by: smittenkittenoriginals

You will need 1 skein of yarn in each of the colors you wish to use and a size J crochet hook

Chain a length that is 5 feet long.

Single crochet across the row. Chain 1, turn, and single crochet back to the beginning, in the front loop only. Chain 2, turn, and double crochet across the row. Chain 2, turn, and double crochet back to the beginning, in the front loop only. Chain 2, turn, and double crochet across the row in the front loop only. Chain 2, turn, and double crochet back to the beginning, in the front loop only.

Chain 2, turn, and double crochet across the row, in the front loop only. Chain 2, turn, and double crochet back to the beginning in the front loop only. Chain 2, turn, and double crochet back to the beginning in the front loop only. Chain 2, turn, and double crochet back to the beginning in the front loop only. Chain 2, turn, and double crochet back to the beginning in the front loop only.

When you are happy with how thick your scarf is, tie it off and add tassels to the ends.

Around the Globe Cowl

Photo made by: smittenkittenoriginals

You will need 1 skein of yarn in each of the colors you wish to use and a size J crochet hook

Chain a length that is 4 feet long.

Single crochet across the row. Chain 1, turn, and single crochet back to the beginning. Chain 1, turn, and single crochet across the row.

Chain 1, turn, and single crochet back to the beginning. Chain 1, turn, and single crochet back to the beginning. Chain 1, turn, and single crochet across the row. Chain 1, turn, and single crochet back to the beginning. Chain 1, turn, and single crochet back to the beginning. Chain 1, turn, and single crochet across the row. Chain 1, turn, and single crochet back to the beginning.

Chain 1, turn, and single crochet across the row. Chain 1, turn, and single crochet back to the beginning. Chain 1, turn, and single crochet back to the beginning. Chain 1, turn, and single crochet across the row. Chain 1, turn, and single crochet back to the beginning. Chain 1, turn, and single crochet back to the beginning. Chain 1, turn, and single crochet across the row. Chain 1, turn, and single crochet back to the beginning.

Continue until the cowl is nice and thick – use the photo for reference. When you are happy with the size of the piece, tie it off.

Sew up the ends of the cowl, and turn the right side out. That's it! You are done!

Super Stripes Autumn Throw

You will need 1 skein of yarn in each of the colors you wish to use and a size J crochet hook

Chain a length that is 5 feet long.

Single crochet across the row. Chain 1, turn, and single crochet back to the beginning. Chain 1, turn, and single crochet across the row. Chain 1, turn, and single crochet back to the beginning. Chain 1, turn, and single crochet back to the beginning. Chain 1, turn, and single crochet across the row. Chain 1, turn, and single crochet back to the beginning. Chain 1, turn, and single crochet back to the beginning. Chain 1, turn, and single crochet across the row. Chain 1, turn, and single crochet back to the beginning.

Use the photo as a reference for color, changing colors as often as you like.

Chain 1, turn, and single crochet across the row. Chain 1, turn, and single crochet back to the beginning. Chain 1, turn, and single crochet back to the beginning. Chain 1, turn, and single crochet across the row. Chain 1, turn, and single crochet back to the beginning. Chain 1, turn, and single crochet back to the beginning. Chain 1, turn, and single crochet across the row. Chain 1, turn, and single crochet back to the beginning.

When you are happy with the size of the blanket, you are going to add a single crochet row around the entire border. Tie off, and you are done!

Every Season Throw

Photo made by: kpwerker

You will need 1 skein of yarn in each of the colors you wish to use and a size J crochet hook

Chain a length that is 8 feet long.

Single crochet across the row. Chain 1, turn, and single crochet back to the beginning. Chain 1, and single crochet in the first 10 stitches, then skip the next stitch. Single crochet in the next 10 stitches, and skip the next stitch. Single crochet in the next 10 stitches, and skip the next stitch. Continue to the end.

Chain 1, and single crochet in the first 10 stitches, then skip the next stitch. Single crochet in the next 10 stitches, and skip the next stitch. Single crochet in the next 10 stitches, and skip the next stitch. Continue to the end.

Chain 1, turn, and single crochet across the row. Chain 1, turn, and single crochet back to the beginning. Chain 1, turn, and single crochet back to the beginning. Chain 1, turn, and single crochet across the row. Chain 1, turn, and single crochet back to the beginning. Chain 1, turn, and single crochet back to the beginning. Chain 1, turn, and single crochet across the row. Chain 1, turn, and single crochet back to the beginning.

Chain 1, turn, and single crochet across the row. Chain 1, turn, and single crochet back to the beginning. Chain 1, turn, and single crochet back to the beginning. Chain 1, turn, and single crochet across the row. Chain 1, turn, and single crochet back to the beginning. Chain 1, turn, and single crochet back to the beginning. Chain 1, turn, and single crochet across the row. Chain 1, turn, and single crochet back to the beginning.

Use the photo as reference, and change colors as much as you like. When you are done, add a border, and enjoy!

Fall Harvest Coasters

Photo made by: <u>hellomomo</u>

You will need 1 skein of yarn in each of the colors you wish to use and a size G crochet hook

Chain 4 and join with a slip stitch to form a ring. Single crochet in the center of this ring 10 times, and join with another slip stitch.

Chain 1, turn, and single crochet around the row. Chain 1, turn, and single crochet back around, joining with a slip stitch when you get back to the beginning. Chain 1, turn, and single crochet back to the beginning. Chain 1, turn, and single crochet back to the beginning, joining with a slip stitch.

Chain 1, turn, and single crochet around the row. Chain 1, turn, and single crochet back around, joining with a slip stitch when you get back to the beginning. Chain 1, turn, and single crochet back to the beginning. Chain 1, turn, and single crochet back to the beginning, joining with a slip stitch.

Chain 1, turn, and single crochet around the row. Chain 1, turn, and single crochet back around, joining with a slip stitch when you get back to the beginning. Chain 1, turn, and single crochet back to the beginning. Chain 1, turn, and single crochet back to the beginning, joining with a slip stitch.

Use short chains of green for the leaves of the fruit, and sew in place.

Continue until you are happy with the size of your coaster, then tie off. Repeat for the other coasters, and you are done!

Droopy Back Beanie

Photo made by: smittenkittenoriginals

You will need 1 skein of yarn in each of the colors you wish to use and a size G crochet hook

Chain 4 and join with a slip stitch to form a ring. Single crochet in the center of this ring 10 times, and join with another slip stitch.

Chain 1, turn, and single crochet around the row. Chain 1, turn, and single crochet back around, joining with a slip stitch when you get back to the beginning. Chain 1, turn, and single crochet back to the beginning. Chain 1, turn, and single crochet back to the beginning, joining with a slip stitch.

Continue with this until you have a disc fits across the top of your head, then begin your decrease.

Chain 1, turn, and single crochet in the first 5 stitches, then skip the next stitch. Single crochet in the next 5 stitches, then skip the next stitch. Single crochet in the next 5 stitches, then skip the next stitch. Single crochet in the next 5 stitches, then skip the next stitch. Single crochet in the next 5 stitches, then skip the next stitch.

Once the hat fits the shape of your head, you are going to work a few rows without decreasing, continuing until the hat is the length that you prefer. Remember that this is a slouchy beanie, so continue until the beanie is long – longer than what you would normally use for a beanie.

Once the hat as reached your desired length, tie off and you are done!

Fall's Fun Fur Scarf

Photo made by: madaise

You will need 1 skein of yarn in each of the colors you wish to use and a size G crochet hook

Chain a length that is 5 inches.

Single crochet across the row. Chain 1, turn, and single crochet back to the beginning. Chain 1, turn, and single crochet across the row. Chain 1, turn, and single crochet back to the beginning. Chain 1, turn, and single crochet back to the beginning. Chain 1, turn, and single crochet across the row. Chain 1, turn, and single crochet back to the beginning. Chain 1, turn, and single crochet back to the beginning. Chain 1, turn, and single crochet across the row. Chain 1, turn, and single crochet back to the beginning.

Chain 1, turn, and single crochet across the row. Chain 1, turn, and single crochet back to the beginning. Chain 1, turn, and single crochet back to the beginning. Chain 1, turn, and single crochet across the row. Chain 1, turn, and single crochet back to the beginning. Chain 1, turn, and single crochet back to the beginning. Chain 1, turn, and single crochet across the row. Chain 1, turn, and single crochet back to the beginning.

When you are happy with the length of the scarf, tie off and you are done!

Pumpkin Spice Scarf

Photo made by: smittenkittenoriginals

You will need 1 skein of yarn in each of the colors you wish to use and a size G crochet hook

Chain a length that is as long as you want your scarf to be.

Single crochet across the row. Chain 1, turn, and single crochet back to the beginning, in the front loop only. Chain 2, turn, and double crochet across the row. Chain 2, turn, and double crochet back to the beginning, in the front loop only. Chain 2, turn, and double crochet across the row in the front loop only. Chain 2, turn, and double crochet back to the beginning, in the front loop only.

Chain 2, turn, and double crochet across the row, in the front loop only. Chain 2, turn, and double crochet back to the beginning in the front loop only. Chain 2, turn, and double crochet back to the beginning in the front loop only. Chain 2, turn, and double crochet back to the beginning in the front loop only. Chain 2, turn, and double crochet back to the beginning in the front loop only. Chain 2, turn, and double crochet back to the beginning in the front loop only.

Change colors as you prefer, using the photo as a reference guide. When you are happy with the size of your scarf, you are done!

Tabletop Owl

Photo made by: Emily Lindberg

You will need 1 skein of yarn in each of the colors you wish to use and a size G crochet hook

Chain 4 and join with a slip stitch to form a ring. Single crochet in the center of this ring 10 times, and join with another slip stitch.

Chain 1, turn, and single crochet around the row. Chain 1, turn, and single crochet back around, joining with a slip stitch when you get back to the beginning. Chain 1, turn, and single crochet back to the beginning. Chain 1, turn, and single crochet back to the beginning, joining with a slip stitch.

Continue with this until you have a disc that is 8 inches across, then begin your decrease.

Chain 1, turn, and single crochet in the first 5 stitches, then skip the next stitch. Single crochet in the next 5 stitches, then skip the next stitch. Single crochet in the next 5 stitches, then skip the next stitch. Single crochet in the next 5 stitches, then skip the next stitch. Single crochet in the next 5 stitches, then skip the next stitch.

Once the owls body is forming, continue with the single crochet rows without any kinds of decreases. When you are happy with the size of the body, you are going to tie off the end and stuff the owl. Sew across the top, forming the shape of your decoration.

Repeat the steps to make 2 discs for eyes, then sew onto the body – following the details that you see in the photo. When you are happy with the final look of the bird, tie off and you are done!

Bright and Bold Pumpkin Scarf

Photo made by: smittenkittenoriginals

You will need 1 skein of yarn in each of the colors you wish to use and a size J crochet hook

Chain a length that is 6 feet long.

Single crochet across the row. Chain 1, turn, and single crochet back to the beginning. Chain 1, turn, and single crochet across the row. Chain 1, turn, and single crochet back to the beginning. Chain 1, turn, and single crochet back to the beginning. Chain 1, turn, and single crochet across the row. Chain 1, turn, and single crochet back to the beginning. Chain 1, turn, and single crochet back to the beginning. Chain 1, turn, and single crochet across the row. Chain 1, turn, and single crochet back to the beginning.

Chain 1, turn, and single crochet across the row. Chain 1, turn, and single crochet back to the beginning. Chain 1, turn, and single crochet back to the beginning. Chain 1, turn, and single crochet across the row. Chain 1, turn, and single crochet back to the beginning. Chain 1, turn, and single crochet back to the beginning. Chain 1, turn, and single crochet across the row. Chain 1, turn, and single crochet back to the beginning.

When you are happy with the thickness of the scarf, tie off and you are done!

Basic Fall Nights Pillow

Photo made by: <u>dainec</u>

You will need 1 skein of yarn in each of the colors you wish to use and a size J crochet hook

Measure a pillow and chain a length that will fit over the side.

Single crochet across the row. Chain 1, turn, and single crochet back to the beginning. Chain 1, turn, and single crochet across the row. Chain 1, turn, and single crochet back to the beginning. Chain 1, turn, and single crochet back to the beginning. Chain 1, turn, and single crochet across the row. Chain 1, turn, and single crochet back to the beginning. Chain 1, turn, and single crochet back to the beginning. Chain 1, turn, and single crochet across the row. Chain 1, turn, and single crochet back to the beginning.

Chain 1, turn, and single crochet across the row. Chain 1, turn, and single crochet back to the beginning. Chain 1, turn, and single crochet back to the beginning. Chain 1, turn, and single crochet across the row. Chain 1, turn, and single crochet back to the beginning. Chain 1, turn, and single crochet back to the beginning. Chain 1, turn, and single crochet across the row. Chain 1, turn, and single crochet back to the beginning.

When you can fit this over your pillow, tie off.

Take your yarn needle now, and sew this around your pillow. Secure an oversized button to the front, and you are done!

Fall Toaster Coasters

Photo made by: Rebecca Kahn

You will need 1 skein of yarn in each of the colors you wish to use and a size G crochet hook

Chain 4 and join with a slip stitch to form a ring. Single crochet in the center of this ring 10 times, and join with another slip stitch.

Chain 1, turn, and single crochet around the row. Chain 1, turn, and single crochet back around, joining with a slip stitch when you get back to the beginning. Chain 1, turn, and single crochet back to the beginning. Chain 1, turn, and single crochet back to the beginning, joining with a slip stitch.

Chain 1, turn, and single crochet around the row. Chain 1, turn, and single crochet back around, joining with a slip stitch when you get back to the beginning. Chain 1, turn, and single crochet back to the beginning. Chain 1, turn, and single crochet back to the beginning, joining with a slip stitch.

Chain 1, turn, and single crochet around the row. Chain 1, turn, and single crochet back around, joining with a slip stitch when you get back to the beginning. Chain 1, turn, and single crochet back to the beginning. Chain 1, turn, and single crochet back to the beginning, joining with a slip stitch.

Continue until you are happy with the size of your coaster, then tie off. Repeat for the other coasters, and you are done!

Fireside Warmth

Photo made by: tonyandshayna

You will need 1 skein of yarn in each of the colors you wish to use and a size J crochet hook

Chain a length that is 6 feet long.

Single crochet across the row. Chain 1, turn, and single crochet back to the beginning, in the front loop only. Chain 2, turn, and double crochet across the row. Chain 2, turn, and double crochet back to the beginning, in the front loop only. Chain 2, turn, and double crochet across the row in the front loop only. Chain 2, turn, and double crochet back to the beginning, in the front loop only.

124

Chain 2, turn, and double crochet across the row, in the front loop only. Chain 2, turn, and double crochet back to the beginning in the front loop only. Chain 2, turn, and double crochet back to the beginning in the front loop only. Chain 2, turn, and double crochet back to the beginning in the front loop only. Chain 2, turn, and double crochet back to the beginning in the front loop only.

Use the photo as a reference for color, changing color as much as you like. Continue to work until your blanket is a square, or until it is the size that you wish it to be. When you are happy with the size, tie off and put a single crochet border around the entire thing.

Tie off the blanket and make sure there are no loose threads, and you are done!

Conclusion

There you have it, everything you need to create a variety of autumn designs, and to make your house cozy and sweet this season! You are going to fall in love with each and every one of these patterns, and you are going to find that each one brings in the joy of the season.

The nights are getting longer, the days are getting colder, and you are ready for the upcoming holidays.

Don't wait – you know this is one of the greatest times of year, and you are going to enjoy each and every second of it. Have fun with your creations, and you are going to embrace all this fall has to offer!

Crochet Bikini For Everyone
5 Masterpiece Crochet Bikinis To Rock On The Beach

Introduction

The sun is out, school is out, and you are due for your summer vacation. Right now, nothing sounds better than sipping on your favorite drink next to a pool or on the beach, or even next to the ocean. Perhaps you have a vacation destination in mind, perhaps you are going to staycation in your own back yard.

No matter what you are going to do, you know you want to look good doing it, and to do that, you are going to need the right swimsuit.

But, bikinis haven't always been your friend. There are times when you felt that you looked good, until you looked in the mirror. There were times when you scoured the shelves of the store to find something that would work for you, but you find that the sets simply don't fit, or the tops or bottoms just don't seem to fit the right way.

So what does that mean? Does that mean that you are stuck with swimsuits that you don't want to wear? Does that mean that you have to suffer through with pieces that you don't think make you look good, or that don't help you to feel good about yourself?

Of course not!

When it comes to swimsuits, you can turn to the world of crochet for your answer.

But, you wonder, isn't it difficult to crochet a bikini? What kind of yarn do you use? How do you know it's going to fit you?

If you have wondered about these things yourself, you have come to the right place. In this book, you are going to discover everything that you need to know to make your own bikinis. You are going to learn the tips and tricks that you need to make swimsuits to fit your body, and you are going to learn how to put in the details that you want.

You are going to get exactly what you want with each and every one of these pieces, and you are going to rock your style on the beach like never before. So what are you waiting for? Grab your favorite cotton yarn, grab your favorite crochet hook, and settle in with a cold glass of iced tea.

You are going to fall in love with the results, and you are going to love each and every piece that you make. There's no end to the wonderful pieces you can make, or how good you can feel when you wear them.

You deserve the best of the best, so let's get started.

Chapter 1 – The Bikini Patterns

Ruby Red Bikini Set

You will need 2 skeins of cotton yarn in ruby red (or the color of your choice) and a size G crochet hook.

For the Top:

Using an unlined bra or a bikini that you already own, chain a length from the top of the cup to the bottom.

Single crochet across the row, and continue to single crochet up and around the top, down to the same point on the other side. Join with a slip stitch, chain 1, turn, and single crochet back around the row. Do not join with a slip stitch this time. Instead, chain 1, turn, and single crochet back to the other side of the row. Again, do not join with a slip stitch. Chain 1, turn, and single crochet back to the beginning.

You are going to see a triangle forming.

Continue to work with this pattern, until you have a cup that is equal to the cup of your bra top or bikini. Tie off the first cup and set aside.

Repeat this for the other cup, then tie off and set aside.

Next, you are going to take your crochet hook and join with a slip stitch to the bottom of one of the cups. Single crochet across this bottom, then continue across the bottom of the other cup. Chain 1, turn, and single crochet back to the beginning. Chain 1, turn, and single crochet back to the other side. Chain 1, turn, and single crochet across the row. Chain 1, turn, and single crochet back to the beginning.

Continue now with this pattern, until you are happy with how far down the piece reaches. Tie off.

Chain 4 chains now, 2 for the neck ties and 2 for the side ties. Single crochet across the row. Chain 1, turn, and single crochet back to the beginning. Tie off each one and set aside.

Attach the chains to the top of the cups, then attach the other two to the sides of the piece. Make sure it is all secure, then you are done! Create 2 tassels using a DVD case, then secure these tassels to the sides of the piece alone

For the Bottoms:

Use either a bikini bottom or a pair of underwear that you already have to get the right size.

Chain a length that is equal to the top of the front of the piece. Chain 1, turn, and single crochet across the row. Chain 1, turn, and single crochet back to the other side. Chain 1, turn, and single crochet across the row. Chain 1, turn, and single crochet back to the other side. Chain 1, turn, and single crochet across the row. Chain 1, turn, and single crochet back to the beginning.

You are going to be using your bikini bottoms or underwear as the template for the piece, and you are going to follow this as a guide for the size of the bottoms.

Following the template, begin to decrease.

Chain 1, skip the first stitch on the row, and single crochet across the row, skipping the last stitch. Chain 1, skip the first stitch on the row, and single crochet across the row, skipping the last stitch. Chain 1, skip the first stitch on the row, and single crochet across the row, skipping the last stitch. Chain 1, skip the first stitch on the row, and single crochet across the row, skipping the last stitch. Chain 1, skip the first stitch on the row, and single crochet across the row, skipping the last stitch.

When you reach the center of the bottoms, you are going to go back to normal crochet, without any decreases:

Chain 1, turn, and single crochet across the row. Chain 1, turn, and single crochet back to the other side. Chain 1, turn, and single crochet across the row. Chain 1, turn, and single crochet back to the other side. Chain 1, turn, and single crochet across the row. Chain 1, turn, and single crochet back to the beginning.

When you get through between your legs, you are going to continue to follow the pattern as you increase once more:

Chain 1 and single crochet in the first stitch 2 times, then single crochet across the row, and single crochet in the last stitch 2 times. Chain 1 and single crochet in the first stitch 2 times, then single crochet across the row, and single crochet in the last stitch 2 times. Chain 1 and single crochet in the first stitch 2 times, then single crochet across the row, and single crochet in the last stitch 2 times.

Continue until you have reached the proper size on the other side. Tie off.

Chain 2 lengths of chain now, 6 inches each. Feed these through the sides of the bottoms, and use as a drawstring when you wear. Create 2 tassels using a DVD case, then secure these tassels to the sides of the bottom of the piece only. Make sure it is all secure, and that there are no loose ends anywhere on the piece. Tie off.

That's it! You're done!

Mesmerizing Pearl Top

You will need 2 skeins of cotton yarn in ivory or off white (or the color of your choice) and a size G crochet hook.

Using an unlined bra or a bikini that you already own, chain a length from the top of the cup to the bottom.

Single crochet across the row, and continue to single crochet up and around the top, down to the same point on the other side. Join with a slip stitch, chain 1, turn, and single crochet back around the row. Do not join with a slip stitch this time. Instead, chain 1, turn, and single crochet back to the other side of the row. Again, do not join with a slip stitch. Chain 1, turn, and single crochet back to the beginning.

You are going to see a triangle forming.

Continue to work with this pattern, until you have a cup that is equal to the cup of your bra top or bikini. Tie off the first cup and set aside.

Repeat this for the other cup, then tie off and set aside.

Next, you are going to take your crochet hook and join with a slip stitch to the bottom of one of the cups. Single crochet across this bottom, then continue across the bottom of the other cup. Chain 1, turn, and single crochet back to the beginning.

For the next row, you are going to chain 5, skip the first 3 stitches, then join with a slip stitch into the next stitch. Chain 5, skip the next 3 stitches, then join with a slip stitch in the next stitch. Chain 5, skip the next 3 stitches, then join with a slip stitch in the next stitch. Chain 5, skip the next 3 stitches, then join with a slip stitch in the next stitch. Chain 5, skip the next 3 stitches, then join with a slip stitch in the next stitch. Repeat this across the row.

For the next row, you are going to chain 5 and join with slip stitch in the middle of the chain space. Chain 5, then join with a slip stitch into the center of the chain space. Chain 5, then join with a slip stitch into the center of the chain space. Chain 5, then join with a slip stitch into the center of the chain space. Chain 5, then join with a slip stitch into the center of the chain space.

Continue now with this pattern, until you are happy with how far down the piece reaches. Tie off.

Chain 4 chains now, 2 for the neck ties and 2 for the side ties. Single crochet across the row. Chain 1, turn, and single crochet back to the beginning. Tie off each one and set aside.

Sew each of these lengths to the cups on the bikini and to the sides, then make sure all is secure. Finish with adding fringe across the front of the piece, using the photo as a reference for placement.

Tie off, and you are done!

Flirty Ruffle Bottoms

You will need 2 skeins of cotton yarn in tan (or the color of your choice) and a size G crochet hook.

Use either a bikini bottom or a pair of underwear that you already have to get the right size.

Chain a length that is equal to the top of the front of the piece. Chain 1, turn, and single crochet across the row. Chain 1, turn, and single crochet back to the other side. Chain 1, turn, and single crochet across the row. Chain 1, turn, and single crochet back to the other side. Chain 1, turn, and single crochet across the row. Chain 1, turn, and single crochet back to the beginning.

You are going to be using your bikini bottoms or underwear as the template for the piece, and you are going to follow this as a guide for the size of the bottoms.

Following the template, begin to decrease.

Chain 1, skip the first stitch on the row, and single crochet across the row, skipping the last stitch. Chain 1, skip the first stitch on the row, and single crochet across the row, skipping the last stitch. Chain 1, skip the first stitch on the row, and single crochet across the row, skipping the last stitch. Chain 1, skip the first stitch on the row, and single crochet across the row, skipping the last stitch. Chain 1, skip the first stitch on the row, and single crochet across the row, skipping the last stitch.

When you reach the center of the bottoms, you are going to go back to normal crochet, without any decreases:

Chain 1, turn, and single crochet across the row. Chain 1, turn, and single crochet back to the other side. Chain 1, turn, and single crochet across the row. Chain 1, turn, and single crochet back to the other side. Chain 1, turn, and single crochet across the row. Chain 1, turn, and single crochet back to the beginning.

When you get through between your legs, you are going to continue to follow the pattern as you increase once more:

Chain 1 and single crochet in the first stitch 2 times, then single crochet across the row, and single crochet in the last stitch 2 times. Chain 1 and single crochet in the first stitch 2 times, then single crochet across the row, and single crochet in the last stitch 2 times. Chain 1 and single crochet in the first stitch 2 times, then single crochet across the row, and single crochet in the last stitch 2 times.

Continue until you have reached the proper size on the other side. Tie off.

Go back to the top now with a contrasting color, and join with a slip stitch. Chain 1, and single crochet in the first stitch. Double crochet in the next 3 stitches, and single crochet in the next stitch. Double crochet in the next 3 stitches, then single crochet in the next stitch. Double crochet in the next 3 stitches, then single crochet in the next stitch. Join both the front and the back this way, working your way around the entire top so the bikini will pull on without strings.

If you would like more security, add a drawstring. Tie off and you are done!

High Wasted Bikini Set

You will need 2 skeins of cotton yarn in grey (or the color of your choice) and a size G crochet hook.

For the Top:

Using an unlined bra or a bikini that you already own, chain a length from the top of the cup to the bottom.

Single crochet across the row, and continue to single crochet up and around the top, down to the same point on the other side. Join with a slip stitch, chain 1, turn, and single crochet back around the row. Do not join with a slip stitch this time. Instead, chain 1, turn, and single crochet back to the other side of the row. Again, do not join with a slip stitch. Chain 1, turn, and single crochet back to the beginning.

You are going to see a triangle forming.

Continue to work with this pattern, until you have a cup that is equal to the cup of your bra top or bikini. Tie off the first cup and set aside.

Repeat this for the other cup, then tie off and set aside.

Next, you are going to take your crochet hook and join with a slip stitch to the bottom of one of the cups. Single crochet across this bottom, then continue across the bottom of the other cup. Chain 1, turn, and single crochet back to the beginning. Chain 1, turn, and single crochet back to the other side. Chain 1, turn, and single crochet across the row. Chain 1, turn, and single crochet back to the beginning.

Continue now with this pattern, until you are happy with how far down the piece reaches. As this is a two piece that is designed to have more coverage than most, you are going to work your way further down the piece than you would with the other pieces. Tie off.

Chain 4 chains now, 2 for the neck ties and 2 for the side ties. Single crochet across the row. Chain 1, turn, and single crochet back to the beginning. Tie off each one and set aside.

Secure these 4 ties to the bikini, making sure they are all sewn securely and will not break off when the bikini is wet. Using a contrasting color, feed this through the bottom part of the piece, adding an accent to the bikini. Tie a bow or allow to hang loose, however you prefer.

That's it! Tie it off and you are done!

For the Bottoms:

Use either a bikini bottom or a pair of underwear that you already have to get the right size.

Chain a length that is equal to the top of the front of the piece. Chain 1, turn, and single crochet across the row. Chain 1, turn, and single crochet back to the other side. Chain 1, turn, and single crochet across the row. Chain 1, turn, and single crochet back to the other side. Chain 1, turn, and single crochet across the row. Chain 1, turn, and single crochet back to the beginning.

Remember you are going to make these high rise, so continue with this pattern until you are happy with the rise of the bottoms.

Just as with other pieces, you are going to be using your bikini bottoms or underwear as the template for the piece, and you are going to follow this as a guide for the size of the bottoms.

When you are happy with the rise, you are going to use the template to begin to decrease.

Chain 1, skip the first stitch on the row, and single crochet across the row, skipping the last stitch. Chain 1, skip the first stitch on the row, and single crochet across the row, skipping the last stitch. Chain 1, skip the first stitch on the row, and single crochet across the row, skipping the last stitch. Chain 1, skip the first stitch on the row, and single crochet across the row, skipping the last stitch. Chain 1, skip the first stitch on the row, and single crochet across the row, skipping the last stitch.

When you reach the center of the bottoms, you are going to go back to normal crochet, without any decreases:

Chain 1, turn, and single crochet across the row. Chain 1, turn, and single crochet back to the other side. Chain 1, turn, and single crochet across the row. Chain 1, turn, and single crochet back to the other side. Chain 1, turn, and single crochet across the row. Chain 1, turn, and single crochet back to the beginning.

When you get through between your legs, you are going to continue to follow the pattern as you increase once more:

Chain 1 and single crochet in the first stitch 2 times, then single crochet across the row, and single crochet in the last stitch 2 times. Chain 1 and single crochet in the first stitch 2 times, then single crochet across the row, and single crochet in the last stitch 2 times. Chain 1 and single crochet in the first stitch 2 times, then single crochet across the row, and single crochet in the last stitch 2 times.

Continue until you have reached the proper size and rise on the other side of the piece. Tie off.

Chain 2 lengths of chain now 1 foot long each. Using the photo as reference, feed these through the sides of the bottoms, and use as a drawstring when you wear.

The Wonder Top + Ruffle Bottoms

You will need 2 skeins of cotton yarn in each of the colors that you choose to use and a size G crochet hook.

If you are going to follow the same color scheme as the photo, you are going to be changing the color of yarn every 2 rows. Pay attention and use the photo as a reference, or simply create your own color scheme.

For the Top:

Using an unlined bra or a bikini that you already own, chain a length from the top of the cup to the bottom.

Single crochet across the row, and continue to single crochet up and around the top, down to the same point on the other side. Join with a slip stitch, chain 1, turn, and single crochet back around the row. Do not join with a slip stitch this time. Instead, chain 1, turn, and single crochet back to the other side of the row. Again, do not join with a slip stitch. Chain 1, turn, and single crochet back to the beginning.

You are going to see a triangle forming. Remember if you are going to be changing colors with this that you need to do so every couple of rows. It's simple to do – all you need to do is tie off the row after 2 rows, then join with the next color. Work 2 rows then tie off, and join with the next color.

Continue to work with this pattern, until you have a cup that is equal to the cup of your bra top or bikini. Tie off the first cup and set aside.

Repeat this for the other cup, then tie off and set aside, once again following the same alternating color pattern as you did in the previous cup, if you chose to stripe your piece.

Now, take your crochet hook and join with a slip stitch on the bottom of one of the cups. Single crochet across the bottom of the row, continuing across the bottom of the second cup, joining the two cups together. Chain 1, turn, and single crochet back to the beginning of the row. Now, you are going to add the ruffle to the bottom of the piece:

Chain 1, and single crochet in the first stitch. Double crochet in the next 3 stitches, and single crochet in the next stitch. Double crochet in the next 3 stitches, then single crochet in the next stitch. Double crochet in the next 3 stitches, then single crochet in the next stitch. Join both the front and the back this way, working your way across the bottom of the piece. Tie off when you reach the beginning.

Chain 4 chains now, 2 for the neck ties and 2 for the side ties. Single crochet across the row. Chain 1, turn, and single crochet back to the beginning. Tie off each one and set aside.

Attach the chains to the top of the cups, then attach the other two to the sides of the piece. Make sure it is all secure, then you are done and ready to head out to rock those waves!

For the Bottoms:

For the ruffle bottoms you are going to follow the same method as before, only if you are going to make them match the top, feel free to stripe them as you did with the top of the piece. Remember to change colors after every couple of rows.

Use either a bikini bottom or a pair of underwear that you already have to get the right size.

Chain a length that is equal to the top of the front of the piece. Chain 1, turn, and single crochet across the row. Chain 1, turn, and single crochet back to the other side. Chain 1, turn, and single crochet across the row. Chain 1, turn, and single crochet back to the other side. Chain 1, turn, and single crochet across the row. Chain 1, turn, and single crochet back to the beginning.

You are going to be using your bikini bottoms or underwear as the template for the piece, and you are going to follow this as a guide for the size of the bottoms.

Following the template, begin to decrease.

Chain 1, skip the first stitch on the row, and single crochet across the row, skipping the last stitch. Chain 1, skip the first stitch on the row, and single crochet across the row, skipping the last stitch. Chain 1, skip the first stitch on the row, and single crochet across the row, skipping the last stitch. Chain 1, skip the first stitch on the row, and single crochet across the row, skipping the last stitch. Chain 1, skip the first stitch on the row, and single crochet across the row, skipping the last stitch.

When you reach the center of the bottoms, you are going to go back to normal crochet, without any decreases:

Chain 1, turn, and single crochet across the row. Chain 1, turn, and single crochet back to the other side. Chain 1, turn, and single crochet across the row. Chain 1, turn, and single crochet back to the other side. Chain 1, turn, and single crochet across the row. Chain 1, turn, and single crochet back to the beginning.

When you get through between your legs, you are going to continue to follow the pattern as you increase once more:

Chain 1 and single crochet in the first stitch 2 times, then single crochet across the row, and single crochet in the last stitch 2 times. Chain 1 and single crochet in the first stitch 2 times, then single crochet across the row, and single crochet in the last stitch 2 times. Chain 1 and single crochet in the first stitch 2 times, then single crochet across the row, and single crochet in the last stitch 2 times.

Continue until you have reached the proper size on the other side. Tie off.

Go back to the top now with a contrasting color, and join with a slip stitch. Chain 1, and single crochet in the first stitch. Double crochet in the next 3 stitches, and single crochet in the next stitch. Double crochet in the next 3 stitches, then single crochet in the next stitch. Double crochet in the next 3 stitches, then single crochet in the next stitch. Join both the front and the back this way, working your way around the entire top so the bikini will pull on without strings. Make sure all is secure, and you are done!

Conclusion

There you have it, everything you need to know to make your own crochet bikinis. You know as soon as summer arrives you are ready to hit the beach, but that can be difficult finding your style in the stores. You don't want to follow what everyone else is doing, you want to show off your own style, and the only way you can do that for sure is to make your own.

I hope you feel inspired by this book, and that you are able to make your own bikini collection to rock this summer. You know you deserve the best of the best, and when you make your own, you are going to ensure you get that very thing. Dive into the world of crochet head first, then dive into the pool head first in your sizzling bikini.

The heat of summer is here already, and you know you are more than ready to hit the beach. So, grab your crochet hook, your favorite kind of yarn (just make sure it's cotton!) and your favorite crochet hook, and you are going to be set for all the heat waves of summer.

Flaunt your bikini body, and show the world what hard work can do. You are one of a kind, you are beautiful, and you have what it takes to turn heads everywhere you go. Whip up a collection of your own bikinis now, and embrace summer for all that you can.

Don't waste these summer months – there's no limit to the number of bikinis you can make, so go wild. Make them in every color of the rainbow, make them in multiple colors themselves. Whatever you do, just make them.

The sky is the limit with your swimsuit collection, and you deserve to have each and every one of these pieces. You work hard for your body, now you need something that fits you in a custom way and shows off each and every one of your curves.

Make the suits to fit you, and forget about trying to fit inside the suits. You can have custom, you can have everything you want, and you can show off your skills to your friends and to the world. Now settle in with your favorite summer beverage, grab your favorite crochet hook, and get ready to show off everything you have worked so hard for.

Happy crocheting.

Crochet Jewelry
20 Crochet Bracelets, Earrings, and Rings You Can Make Yourself!

Introduction

Every day is a good day to set a new trend, and you are always ready to strut your stuff. But, this isn't always easy when you have a limited selection of items to choose from.

Sure, you can mix and match, but how many times can you do that without being bored? You want something new and exciting. You want something that makes you feel amazing as you walk down the street, and you want something that is going to show the world that you know how to set trends, and you aren't afraid to do it.

But, you feel overwhelmed.

Where do you start?

How do you know you are going to get the pieces that you want?

How to you express your style when you feel like you've hit a creative roadblock?

If you have been feeling this way, you have come to the right place. In this book, you are going to learn everything you need to know to create your own jewelry pieces, and to show off to the world your own unique style. Whether you choose to make these each as they are exactly, or you take what you see here and turn them into something that is your own, you are going to find that making your own jewelry line is easier than ever.

This book is going to give you everything you need to crochet your own jewelry pieces, and you are going to find the inspiration to be endless. So go ahead, put on your own creative thinking cap, and get ready to dive into a new world of jewelry and trends like you have never imagined before.

There's no way you can do it wrong when you are happy with the results, and this book is the little push you need to get there. Settle in with your favorite crochet hook, your favorite color yarn, and a glass of your favorite ice cold beverage, and you are going to get everything you have ever wanted for your accessory collection.

Get ready to dive into the world of fashion design, and learn for yourself what it feels like to create pieces that you are happy to show off to the world. You know you want to, so don't let anything hold you back.

Let's get started.

Chapter 1 – Crochet Earrings

Red as a Ruby Dangle Earrings

Photo made by: kaylkels

You will need:

Earring hooks

Size E crochet hook

Needle and thread

Jewelry wire

Thread yarn

Directions:

Chain 14 and join with a slip stitch to form a ring.

Single crochet in the center of this ring 16 times, and join with a slip stitch. Chain 1, turn, and single crochet back to the other side. Join with a slip stitch. Chain 1, turn, and single crochet back to the beginning. Join with a slip stitch.

Continue until you are happy with the size of the earring, then finish with a border.

To shape the petals, you are going to:

Chain 3 and skip the first 2 stitches, then join with a slip stitch in the next stitch. Chain 3 and skip the next 2 stitches, then join with a slip stitch in the next stitch. Chain 3 and skip the next 2 stitches, and join with a slip stitch in the next stitch. Repeat around.

Repeat for the other earring.

To assemble:

Using the photo as a reference, assemble your earrings as you see here. Use tight, even stitches as you work, ensuring that none of the wire shows through the piece.

Tie off, and cut off all the loose threads. That's it!

Key Lime Earring Set

Photo made by: moiracrochetsplarn

You will need:

Earring hooks

Size E crochet hook

Needle and thread

Cross Beads

Thin lengths of plastic in the color of your choice (cut up plastic bags work well)

Directions:

Chain 4 and join with a slip stitch to form a ring.

Single crochet in the center of this ring 8 times, and join with a slip stitch. Chain 1, turn, and single crochet back to the other side. Join with a slip stitch. Chain 1, turn, and single crochet back to the beginning. Join with a slip stitch. Chain 1, turn, and single crochet back to the other side.

Continue until you are happy with the size of the earring, then finish with a border.

Repeat for the other earring.

To assemble:

Using the photo as a reference, assemble your earrings as you see here. Use tight, even stitches as you work, ensuring that none of the wire shows through the piece. Attach the beads as you see in the photo as well.

Tie off, and cut off all the loose threads. That's it!

All the Gum Drops Earrings

Photo made by: moiracrochetsplarn

You will need:

Earring hooks

Size E crochet hook

Needle and thread

Thin lengths of plastic in the color of your choice (cut up plastic bags work well)

Directions:

Chain 4 and join with a slip stitch to form a ring.

Single crochet in the center of this ring 8 times, and join with a slip stitch. Chain 1, turn, and single crochet back to the other side. Join with a slip stitch. Chain 1, turn, and single crochet back to the beginning. Join with a slip stitch. Chain 1, turn, and single crochet back to the other side.

Continue until you are happy with the size of the earring, then tie off.

Repeat for the other earring.

To assemble:

Using the photo as a reference, assemble your earrings as you see here. Use tight, even stitches as you work, ensuring that none of the wire shows through the piece.

Tie off, and cut off all the loose threads. That's it!

Bleeding Heart Earrings

Photo made by: moiracrochetsplarn

You will need:

Earring hooks

Size E crochet hook

Needle and thread

Thin lengths of plastic in the color of your choice (cut up plastic bags work well)

Directions:

Chain 4 and join with a slip stitch to form a ring.

Single crochet in the center of this ring 8 times, and join with a slip stitch. Chain 1, turn, and single crochet back to the other side. Join with a slip stitch. Chain 1, turn, and single crochet back to the beginning. Join with a slip stitch. Chain 1, turn, and single crochet back to the other side.

Continue until you are happy with the size of the earring, then finish with a border.

To shape the petals, you are going to:

Chain 5 and skip the first 2 stitches, then join with a slip stitch in the next stitch. Chain 5 and skip the next 2 stitches, then join with a slip stitch in the next stitch. Chain 5 and skip the next 2 stitches, and join with a slip stitch in the next stitch. Repeat around.

Repeat for the other earrings, adjusting the size according to the photo.

To assemble:

Using the photo as a reference, assemble your earrings as you see here. Use tight, even stitches as you work, ensuring that none of the wire shows through the piece.

Tie off, and cut off all the loose threads. That's it!

Hoops and Swoops Earrings

Photo made by: Maria Panayiotou

You will need:

Earring hooks

Size E crochet hook

Needle and thread

Jewelry wire

Thread weight yarn in the color of your choice

Directions:

Decide how large you want the finished piece to be, then chain a length that is equal to this measurement. Single crochet across the row. Chain 1, turn, and single crochet back to the other side. Chain 1, turn, and single crochet back to the beginning. Chain 1, turn, and single crochet back to the other side. Chain 1, turn, and single crochet back to the beginning.

You are going to continue with this until the strip that you create is large enough to wrap entirely around the wire you have chosen. When you are happy with the size, tie off.

Repeat for the other earring.

To assemble:

Using the photo as a reference, assemble your earrings as you see here. Use tight, even stitches as you work, ensuring that none of the wire shows through the piece.

Tie off, and cut off all the loose threads. That's it!

Mottled Magic Earrings

Photo made by: moiracrochetsplarn

You will need:

Earring hooks

Size E crochet hook

Needle and thread

Thin lengths of plastic in the color of your choice (cut up plastic bags work well)

Directions:

Chain 4 and join with a slip stitch to form a ring.

Single crochet in the center of this ring 8 times, and join with a slip stitch. Chain 1, turn, and single crochet back to the other side. Join with a slip stitch. Chain 1, turn, and single crochet back to the beginning. Join with a slip stitch. Chain 1, turn, and single crochet back to the other side.

Continue until you are happy with the size of the earring, then finish with a border.

To shape the petals, you are going to:

Chain 5 and skip the first 2 stitches, then join with a slip stitch in the next stitch. Chain 5 and skip the next 2 stitches, then join with a slip stitch in the next stitch. Chain 5 and skip the next 2 stitches, and join with a slip stitch in the next stitch. Repeat around.

Repeat for the other earring.

To assemble:

Using the photo as a reference, assemble your earrings as you see here. Use tight, even stitches as you work, ensuring that none of the wire shows through the piece.

Tie off, and cut off all the loose threads. That's it!

Star of the Show Earring Set

Photo made by: mccordworks

You will need:

Earring hooks

Size E crochet hook

Needle and thread

Jewelry wire

Thin lengths of plastic in the color of your choice (cut up plastic bags work well)

Directions:

Chain 4 and join with a slip stitch to form a ring.

Single crochet in the center of this ring 8 times, and join with a slip stitch. Chain 1, turn, and single crochet back to the other side. Join with a slip stitch. Chain 1, turn, and single crochet back to the beginning.

Continue until you are happy with the size of the earring, then finish with a border.

To shape the petals, you are going to:

Chain 5 and skip the first 2 stitches, then join with a slip stitch in the next stitch. Slip stitch down the side of the circle until you are ready to form another point. Chain 5 and skip the next 2 stitches, then join with a slip stitch in the next stitch.

Slip stitch down the side of the piece until you are ready to make another point. Chain 5 and skip the next 2 stitches, and join with a slip stitch in the next stitch.

Repeat around. When you are finished, tie off.

Repeat for the other earring.

To assemble:

Using the photo as a reference, assemble your earrings as you see here. Use tight, even stitches as you work, ensuring that none of the wire shows through the piece.

Tie off, and cut off all the loose threads. That's it!

Chapter 2 – Crochet Bracelets

Sea Bracelet

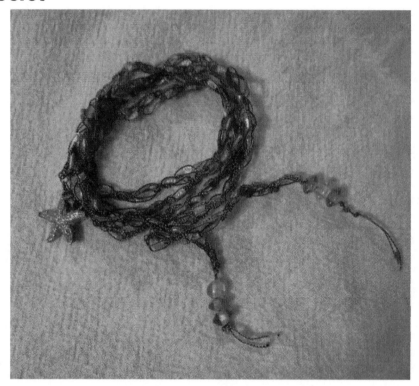

Photo made by: wisewellwoman

What you will need:

Size E crochet hook

Beads

Charms

Needle and thread

Thread weight yarn of your choice

Directions:

Decide how large you want the finished piece to be, then chain a length that is equal to this measurement. Single crochet across the row. Chain 1, turn, and single crochet back to the other side.

This is going to remain a thin length of chain, as you are going to then wrap it around the beads you have selected. After you are happy with how long and thick the first piece is, and you know it's going to fit the beads, you are going to tie off and set it aside.

Chain another length that is equal to the first. Single crochet across the row. Chain 1, turn, and single crochet back to the other side.

Once again, this is going to remain a thin length of chain, as you are going to then wrap it around the beads you have selected. After you are happy with how long and thick the first piece is, and you know it's going to fit the beads, you are going to tie off and set it aside.

Once more, chain another length that is equal to the first. Single crochet across the row. Chain 1, turn, and single crochet back to the other side.

When you have finished the three chains, you are ready to assemble.

To assemble:

Use the photo as a reference for assembly, and don't be afraid to throw in some of your own creativity. Intertwine the pieces together, make sure they are all secure, and attach any and all charms that you wish to be on your piece.

When you are happy with how it looks, snip off any loose ends, and attach a clasp, if desired.

That's it!

It's All in the Braid

Photo made by: tafkabecky

What you will need:

Size E crochet hook

Needle and thread

Thread weight yarn of your choice

Directions:

Decide how large you want the finished piece to be, then chain a length that is equal to this measurement. Single crochet across the row. Chain 1, turn, and single crochet back to the other side.

This is going to remain a thin length of chain, as you are going to braid them together when you are done. After you are happy with how long and thick the first piece is, you are going to tie off and set it aside.

Chain another length that is equal to the first. Single crochet across the row. Chain 1, turn, and single crochet back to the other side.

Once again, this is going to remain a thin length of chain, as you are going to braid them together when you are done. After you are happy with how long and thick the first piece is, you are going to tie off and set it aside.

Once more, chain another length that is equal to the first. Single crochet across the row. Chain 1, turn, and single crochet back to the other side.

When you have finished the three chains, you are ready to assemble.

To assemble:

Use the photo as a reference for assembly, and don't be afraid to throw in some of your own creativity. Intertwine the pieces together, make sure they are all secure, and attach any and all charms that you wish to be on your piece.

When you are happy with how it looks, snip off any loose ends, and attach a clasp, if desired.

And you are done!

The Cage of Glory Bracelet

Photo made by: moiracrochetsplarn

What you will need:

Size E crochet hook

Thin plastic strips – cutting up a plastic bag works well.

Needle and thread

Directions:

Chain 12.

Single crochet across the row. Chain 16 now, and join with a slip stitch to the opposite side of the bracelet. Single crochet in the first stitch. Chain 16 once more, and join with a slip stitch to the other side of the bracelet. Single crochet in the first stitch.

Continue until the bracelet can fit around your wrist, then assemble.

To assemble:

Use the photo as a reference for assembly, and don't be afraid to throw in some of your own creativity. Intertwine the pieces together, make sure they are all secure, and attach any and all charms that you wish to be on your piece.

When you are happy with how it looks, snip off any loose ends, and attach a clasp, if desired.

That's it! You're done!

It's Hip to be a Square

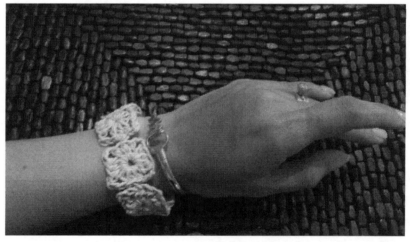

Photo made by: tracey leigh

What you will need:

Size E crochet hook

Thread weight yarn in the color of your choice

Needle and thread

Directions:

Chain 4 and join with a slip stitch to form a ring.

Single crochet in the center of this ring 8 times, and join with a slip stitch. Chain 1, turn, and single crochet back to the other side. Join with a slip stitch. Chain 1, turn, and single crochet back to the beginning. Join with a slip stitch. Chain 1, turn, and single crochet back to the other side.

Continue until you are happy with the size of the center.

To form the square shape, you are going to single crochet across the top, then chain 3 before continuing to single crochet in the very next stitch. This will form the angle. Single crochet across the side and chain 3 to form the next angle. Repeat for the other two sides.

Work 1 more row of single crochet, following your new pattern. Tie off and repeat until you have enough squares to fit around your wrist.

To assemble:

Use the photo as a reference for assembly, and don't be afraid to throw in some of your own creativity. Intertwine the pieces together, make sure they are all secure, and attach any and all charms that you wish to be on your piece.

When you are happy with how it looks, snip off any loose ends, and attach a clasp, if desired.

That's it, your new bracelet is ready for anything!

The Simple Solution

Photo made by: mariatenorio

What you will need:

Size E crochet hook

Thread weight yarn in the color of your choice

Needle and thread

Directions:

Decide how large you want the finished piece to be, then chain a length that is equal to this measurement. Single crochet across the row. Chain 1, turn, and single crochet back to the other side.

This is going to remain a thin length of chain, as you are going to sew them together when you are done. After you are happy with how long and thick the first piece is, you are going to tie off and set it aside.

Chain another length that is equal to the first. Single crochet across the row. Chain 1, turn, and single crochet back to the other side.

Once again, this is going to remain a thin length of chain, as you are going to sewing it to the other strip. After you are happy with how long and thick the first piece is, you are going to tie off.

To assemble:

Use the photo as a reference for assembly, and don't be afraid to throw in some of your own creativity. Intertwine the pieces together, make sure they are all secure, and attach any and all charms that you wish to be on your piece.

When you are happy with how it looks, snip off any loose ends, and attach a clasp, if desired.

That's it!

Sunny Day Bracelet

Photo made by: nikijulian

What you will need:

Size G crochet hook

Large button

Cotton yarn in the color of your choice

Needle and thread

Directions:

Decide how large you want the finished piece to be, then chain a length that is equal to this measurement. Single crochet across the row. Chain 1, turn, and single crochet back to the other side. Chain 1, turn, and single crochet back to the beginning. Chain 1, turn, and single crochet back to the other side. Chain 1, turn, and single crochet back to the beginning.

When you are happy with how thick the strip is, you are going to tie it off. You are now ready to assemble.

To assemble:

Use the photo as a reference for assembly, and don't be afraid to throw in some of your own creativity. Intertwine the pieces together, make sure they are all secure, and attach any and all charms that you wish to be on your piece.

When you are happy with how it looks, snip off any loose ends, and attach a clasp, if desired.

That's it! You can leave it as it is, or add more buttons to it if you like, get creative!

Fall Fantasy Bracelet

Photo made by: reginarioux

What you will need:

Size E crochet hook

Needle and thread

Thread weight yarn in the color of your choice

Bangle wire or jewelry wire you can bend to fit your wrist

Directions:

Start with chaining a length that is as long as you want the feather to be – about 2 inches is standard. Tie off and set aside.

Next, begin chaining shorter lengths, tying each one off and setting it aside when you are happy with the size. Make the lengths that are closer to the top of the feather longer than the lengths that are at the tip, forming the feather shape.

Use the photo as reference.

To assemble:

Use the photo as a reference for assembly, and don't be afraid to throw in some of your own creativity. Intertwine the pieces together, make sure they are all secure, and attach any and all charms that you wish to be on your piece.

When you are happy with how it looks, snip off any loose ends, and attach a clasp, if desired.

That's it! Try making the bracelet over again in as many colors as you can think of!

Chapter 3 – Crochet Rings

The Simple Things Ring

Photo made by: poptoplady

What you will need:

Size E crochet hook

Thread weight yarn in the color of your choice

Soda caps

Needle and thread

Directions:

Chain 4 and join with a slip stitch to form a ring.

Single crochet in the center of this ring 8 times, and join with a slip stitch. Chain 1, turn, and single crochet back to the other side. Join with a slip stitch. Chain 1, turn, and single crochet back to the beginning. Join with a slip stitch. Chain 1, turn, and single crochet back to the other side.

When you are happy with the size of the center, take your soda caps and lay them as you see in the photo. You are ready to assemble.

To assemble:

Use the photo as a reference for assembly, and don't be afraid to throw in some of your own creativity. Intertwine the pieces together, make sure they are all secure, and attach any and all charms that you wish to be on your piece.

When you are happy with how it looks, take a length of thread, a crocheted chain, wire, or metal chain and cut it to the proper length to fit around your finger. Sew the main pendant of the piece to this length, and make sure you have all pieces entirely secure.

When you are happy with how it looks, you are ready to rock your new style!

The Fairy Garden Ring

Photo made by: kaylkels

What you will need:

Size E crochet hook

Thread weight yarn in the color of your choice

Needle and thread

Directions:

Chain 4 and join with a slip stitch to form a ring.

Single crochet in the center of this ring 8 times, and join with a slip stitch. Chain 1, turn, and single crochet back to the other side. Join with a slip stitch. Chain 1, turn, and single crochet back to the beginning. Join with a slip stitch. Chain 1, turn, and single crochet back to the other side.

Continue until you are happy with the size of the earring, then finish with a border.

To shape the petals, you are going to:

Chain 4 and skip the first 2 stitches, then join with a slip stitch in the next stitch. Chain 4 and skip the next 2 stitches, then join with a slip stitch in the next stitch. Chain 4 and skip the next 2 stitches, and join with a slip stitch in the next stitch. Repeat around.

To assemble:

Use the photo as a reference for assembly, and don't be afraid to throw in some of your own creativity. Intertwine the pieces together, make sure they are all secure, and attach any and all charms that you wish to be on your piece.

When you are happy with how it looks, crochet a length that will fit around your finger. Single crochet across the row. Chain 1, turn, and single crochet back to the beginning. Chain 1, turn, and single crochet back to the other side. Chain 1, turn, and single crochet back to the beginning.

Continue until you are happy with how the wrap looks around your finger, then tie off. You can make this as thin or as thick as you like.

When you are happy with how it looks, you are ready to rock your new style!

Barely There White Ring

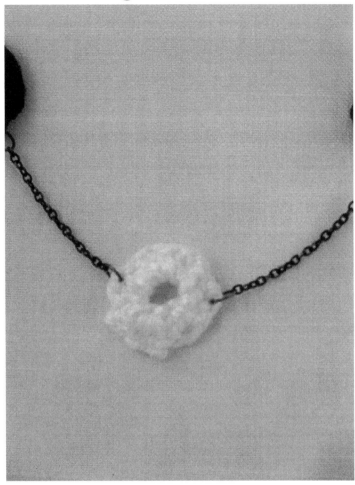

Photo made by: anniehp

What you will need:

Size E crochet hook

Thread weight yarn in the color of your choice

Needle and thread

Directions:

Chain 4 and join with a slip stitch to form a ring.

Single crochet in the center of this ring 8 times, and join with a slip stitch. Chain 1, turn, and single crochet back to the other side. Join with a slip stitch. Chain 1, turn, and single crochet back to the beginning. Join with a slip stitch. Chain 1, turn, and single crochet back to the other side.

Continue until you are happy with the size of the earring, tie off.

To assemble:

Use the photo as a reference for assembly, and don't be afraid to throw in some of your own creativity. Intertwine the pieces together, make sure they are all secure, and attach any and all charms that you wish to be on your piece.

When you are happy with how it looks, take a length of thread, a crocheted chain, wire, or metal chain and cut it to the proper length to fit around your finger. Sew the main pendant of the piece to this length, and make sure you have all pieces entirely secure.

When you are happy with how it looks, you are ready to rock your new style!

The Oversized Statement Ring

Photo made by: sionakaren

What you will need:

Size E crochet hook

Thread weight yarn in the color of your choice

Needle and thread

Directions:

Chain 4 and join with a slip stitch to form a ring.

Single crochet in the center of this ring 8 times, and join with a slip stitch. Chain 1, turn, and single crochet back to the other side. Join with a slip stitch. Chain 1, turn, and single crochet back to the beginning. Join with a slip stitch. Chain 1, turn, and single crochet back to the other side.

Continue until you are happy with the size of the earring, then finish with a border.

To shape the petals, you are going to:

Chain 10 and skip the first 2 stitches, then join with a slip stitch in the next stitch. Chain 10 and skip the next 2 stitches, then join with a slip stitch in the next stitch. Chain 10 and skip the next 2 stitches, and join with a slip stitch in the next stitch. Repeat around.

To assemble:

Use the photo as a reference for assembly, and don't be afraid to throw in some of your own creativity. Intertwine the pieces together, make sure they are all secure, and attach any and all charms that you wish to be on your piece.

When you are happy with how it looks, take a length of thread, a crocheted chain, wire, or metal chain and cut it to the proper length to fit around your finger. Sew the main pendant of the piece to this length, and make sure you have all pieces entirely secure.

When you are happy with how it looks, you are ready to rock your new style!

The Plum Summer Ring

Photo made by: sammy4586

What you will need:

Size E crochet hook

Thread weight yarn in the color of your choice

Needle and thread

Directions:

Chain 4 and join with a slip stitch to form a ring.

Single crochet in the center of this ring 8 times, and join with a slip stitch. Chain 1, turn, and single crochet back to the other side. Join with a slip stitch. Chain 1, turn, and single crochet back to the beginning. Join with a slip stitch. Chain 1, turn, and single crochet back to the other side.

Continue until you are happy with the size of the earring, then finish with a border.

To shape the petals, you are going to:

Chain 4 and skip the first 2 stitches, then join with a slip stitch in the next stitch. Chain 4 and skip the next 2 stitches, then join with a slip stitch in the next stitch. Chain 4 and skip the next 2 stitches, and join with a slip stitch in the next stitch. Repeat around.

To assemble:

Use the photo as a reference for assembly, and don't be afraid to throw in some of your own creativity. Intertwine the pieces together, make sure they are all secure, and attach any and all charms that you wish to be on your piece.

When you are happy with how it looks, take a length of thread, a crocheted chain, wire, or metal chain and cut it to the proper length to fit around your finger. Sew the main pendant of the piece to this length, and make sure you have all pieces entirely secure.

When you are happy with how it looks, you are ready to rock your new style!

Oh So Tiny Ring

Photo made by: nicasaurusrex

What you will need:

Size E crochet hook

Thread weight yarn in the color of your choice

Needle and thread

Directions:

Chain 4 and join with a slip stitch to form a ring.

Single crochet in the center of this ring 4 times, and join with a slip stitch. Chain 1, turn, and single crochet back to the other side. Join with a slip stitch. Chain 1, turn, and single crochet back to the beginning.

Continue until you are happy with the size of the earring, then finish with a border.

To shape the petals, you are going to:

Chain 3 and skip the first stitch, then join with a slip stitch in the next stitch. Chain 3 and skip the next stitch, then join with a slip stitch in the next stitch. Chain 3 and skip the next stitch, and join with a slip stitch in the next stitch. Repeat around.

To assemble:

Use the photo as a reference for assembly, and don't be afraid to throw in some of your own creativity. Intertwine the pieces together, make sure they are all secure, and attach any and all charms that you wish to be on your piece.

When you are happy with how it looks, take a length of thread, a crocheted chain, wire, or metal chain and cut it to the proper length to fit around your finger. Sew the main pendant of the piece to this length, and make sure you have all pieces entirely secure.

When you are happy with how it looks, you are ready to rock your new style!

Conclusion

There you have it, everything you need to know about making your own crochet jewelry, and a variety of patterns you can choose from to rock your style today. I hope this book is able to inspire you to create your very own jewelry collection, and that you take what you have learned here and create all kinds of pieces for your accessory needs.

There is no end to the ways you can create your own jewelry, or to how you can express your creativity while you do it. Have fun, show off your skills, and wow your friends and family with your new accessories every time you see them.

You know you want to, and now it's never been easier to do that very thing. You can be a fashion designer, you can get exactly what you want, when you want it, and you can do it all on your own.

Good luck!

Crochet Projects In One Hour
15 Adorable Ideas For Everyone Who Loves Crocheting But Has No Time!

Introduction

You spend your day running around like a busy bee, trying to get everything done, and make sure everyone in your family is fed, healthy, and happy. By the end of the night, you are so tired you don't want to start a big project, although you do find crochet to be incredibly relaxing.

But you don't want to start something now that you know is going to take you months to complete. And you don't want to get into something that is going to require as much effort out of you as the daily duties that crop up. You want something that you can do quickly and easily, and something that will give you an actual project when you are done.

If this sounds like you, then you have come to the right place. This book is full of many different crochet patterns, and each one can be completed in an hour or less. There's no need to worry or stress that you are going to have to commit to a big project, because these projects are going to give you the results that you want in a matter of minutes.

Think of it as the best of both worlds, and you are going to get the projects you want every time you sit down to crochet. Last minute gifts? Only have a few minutes to sit down and you want to spend it doing something with your hands?

Want to make something quickly while you relax?

If you answered 'yes' to any of those questions, then you are going to be thrilled with the items you find in this book. There's no end to the ways you can make them your own, and in no time at all, you're going to have settled into a new kind of routine.

Make the patterns as they are, or throw in your own creativity with size, texture, and color, and you are going to have the solution to every five minute project you have ever wanted to make.

You live a busy life, but you deserve a few minutes to yourself. Grab your favorite yarn and your collection of crochet hooks and put your feet up.

Let's get started.

Chapter 1 – The Projects

Winter Sunset Crochet Headband

Photo made by: <u>peregrine blue</u>

You will need 1 skein of yarn in multi-color and a size J crochet hook

Chain a length that is 5 inches long.

Single crochet across the row. Chain 1, turn, and single crochet back to the beginning, in the front loop only. Chain 1, turn, and single crochet back to the other side of the row, again in the front loop only. Chain 1, turn, and single crochet across the row in the front loop only. Chain 1, turn, and single crochet back to the beginning in the front loop only.

Chain 1, turn, and single crochet across the row, in the front loop only. Chain 1, turn, and single crochet back to the beginning, in the front loop only. Chain 1, turn, and single crochet back to the other side of the row, again in the front loop only. Chain 1, turn, and single crochet across the row in the front loop only. Chain 1, turn, and single crochet back to the beginning in the front loop only.

Chain 1, turn, and single crochet across the row, in the front loop only. Chain 1, turn, and single crochet back to the beginning, in the front loop only. Chain 1, turn, and single crochet back to the other side of the row, again in the front loop only. Chain 1, turn, and single crochet across the row in the front loop only. Chain 1, turn, and single crochet back to the beginning in the front loop only.

Measure as you go, and keep an eye on your tension. When the piece can reach comfortably around your head, tie off.

Take your yarn needle now, and sew up the open end of the headband. Use a whip stitch and make sure all is secure, then tie off.

That's it! your headband is done!

The Mandala Vase Holder

Photo made by: peregrineblue

You will need 1 skein of yarn in multi-color and a size J crochet hook

Chain 4 and join with a slip stitch to form a ring. Single crochet in the center of this ring 10 times, and join with a slip stitch.

Chain 1, turn, and single crochet around the row, joining with a slip stitch. Chain 1, turn, and single crochet back around to the other side, and join with a slip stitch. Chain 1, turn, and single crochet back to the beginning, joining with a slip stitch. Chain 1, turn, and single crochet back to the other side, joining with a slip stitch.

Chain 1, turn, and single crochet around the row, joining with a slip stitch. Chain 1, turn, and single crochet back around to the other side, and join with a slip stitch. Chain 1, turn, and single crochet back to the beginning, joining with a slip stitch. Chain 1, turn, and single crochet back to the other side, joining with a slip stitch.

Continue until you are happy with the size of your vase base, then tie off, and you are done!

Mandala Wall Art

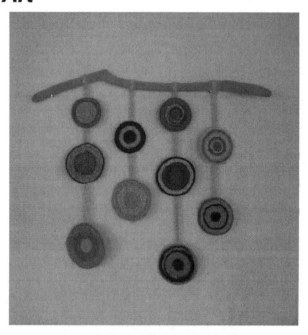

Photo made by: peregrineblue

You will need scrap yarn or 1 skein of yarn in multi-color and a size G crochet hook

You are going to make a total of 10 mandalas, choosing the colors you prefer. Make each one the size you wish for it to be, and tie off and set aside each one as it is completed.

Chain 4 and join with a slip stitch to form a ring. Single crochet in the center of this ring 10 times, and join with a slip stitch.

Chain 1, turn, and single crochet around the row, joining with a slip stitch. Chain 1, turn, and single crochet back around to the other side, and join with a slip stitch. Chain 1, turn, and single crochet back to the beginning, joining with a slip stitch. Chain 1, turn, and single crochet back to the other side, joining with a slip stitch.

Chain 1, turn, and single crochet around the row, joining with a slip stitch. Chain 1, turn, and single crochet back around to the other side, and join with a slip stitch. Chain 1, turn, and single crochet back to the beginning, joining with a slip stitch. Chain 1, turn, and single crochet back to the other side, joining with a slip stitch.

Tie off each one and set aside when you are happy with the size.

Once you have created all the mandalas, you are going to chain 3 or 4 different lengths of chain, and single crochet across the row for a total of 3 rows each. Secure them to your wall mount, and sew each of the mandalas onto the chains.

The Springtime Skinny Scarf

Photo made by: elainegreycats

You will need 1 skein of yarn in the color of your choice and a size J crochet hook

Chain a length that is 4 inches long.

Single crochet across the row. Chain 1, turn, and single crochet back to the beginning. Chain 1, turn, and single crochet across the row. Chain 1, turn, and single crochet back to the beginning. Chain 1, turn, and single crochet across the row. Chain 1, turn, and single crochet back to the beginning.

Single crochet across the row. Chain 1, turn, and single crochet back to the beginning. Chain 1, turn, and single crochet across the row. Chain 1, turn, and single crochet back to the beginning. Chain 1, turn, and single crochet across the row. Chain 1, turn, and single crochet back to the beginning.

Single crochet across the row. Chain 1, turn, and single crochet back to the beginning. Chain 1, turn, and single crochet across the row. Chain 1, turn, and single crochet back to the beginning. Chain 1, turn, and single crochet across the row. Chain 1, turn, and single crochet back to the beginning.

Continue for as long as you want your scarf to be. When you are happy with the length, chain 5, and skip the next 2 stitches, and join with a slip stitch in the next stitch. Chain 5, skip the next 2 stitches, and join with a slip stitch into the next stitch. Chain 5, and skip the next 2 stitches, and join with a slip stitch into the next stitch.

Repeat this around the entire border, and you are done!

Fast and Easy Crochet Cuff

Photo made by: rankinmiss

You will need 1 skein of yarn in the color of your choice and a size G crochet hook

Measure around your wrist, and chain a length that is equal to this measurement. This can either be loose enough to slip over your hand, or snug fitting with a clasp.

Single crochet across the row. Chain 5, turn, and skip the first 2 stitches, then work a slip stitch into the next stitch. Chain 5, skip the next 2 stitches, and work a slip stitch into the next stitch. Continue across the row.

Chain 5, and join with a slip stitch in the center of the chain space. Chain 5, and join with a slip stitch in the center of the chain space. Chain 5, and join with a slip stitch in the center of the chain space. Continue across the row.

Chain 1, turn. Single crochet across the row. Chain 1, turn. Single crochet across the row.

Tie off, and assemble according to your preference.

That's it! Your cuff is ready to rock and roll!

Waste Basket Camo Cover

Photo made by: tterragpics

You will need 1 skein of yarn in the color of your choice and a size J crochet hook

Chain 4 and join with a slip stitch to form a ring. Single crochet in the center of this ring 10 times, and join with a slip stitch.

Chain 1, turn, and single crochet around the row, joining with a slip stitch. Chain 1, turn, and single crochet back around to the other side, and join with a slip stitch. Chain 1, turn, and single crochet back to the beginning, joining with a slip stitch. Chain 1, turn, and single crochet back to the other side, joining with a slip stitch.

Chain 1, turn, and single crochet around the row, joining with a slip stitch. Chain 1, turn, and single crochet back around to the other side, and join with a slip stitch. Chain 1, turn, and single crochet back to the beginning, joining with a slip stitch. Chain 1, turn, and single crochet back to the other side, joining with a slip stitch.

When you are happy with the size of the base, you are going to begin with the decrease row.

Chain 1, and single crochet in the first 4 stitches, then skip the next stitch. Single crochet in the next 4 stitches, and skip the next stitch. Single crochet in the next 4 stitches, and skip the next stitch. Repeat this around.

Work 1 more decrease row.

Now, continue to work your way up the side of the cover, until you are happy with the overall size of the piece.

Chain 1, turn, and single crochet around the row, joining with a slip stitch. Chain 1, turn, and single crochet back around to the other side, and join with a slip stitch. Chain 1, turn, and single crochet back to the beginning, joining with a slip stitch. Chain 1, turn, and single crochet back to the other side, joining with a slip stitch.

Chain 1, turn, and single crochet around the row, joining with a slip stitch. Chain 1, turn, and single crochet back around to the other side, and join with a slip stitch. Chain 1, turn, and single crochet back to the beginning, joining with a slip stitch. Chain 1, turn, and single crochet back to the other side, joining with a slip stitch.

Once the cover is the right height, tie off.

Chain a length that will reach around the entire cover, then use your yarn needle to carefully feed this through the top of the basket. Tie off, and you are done!

A Fairy Trinket Bag

Photo made by: dsoltesz

You will need 1 skein of yarn in the color of your choice and a size G crochet hook

Chain 4 and join with a slip stitch to form a ring. Single crochet in the center of this ring 10 times, and join with a slip stitch.

Chain 1, turn, and single crochet around the row, joining with a slip stitch. Chain 1, turn, and single crochet back around to the other side, and join with a slip stitch. Chain 1, turn, and single crochet back to the beginning, joining with a slip stitch. Chain 1, turn, and single crochet back to the other side, joining with a slip stitch.

Chain 1, turn, and single crochet around the row, joining with a slip stitch. Chain 1, turn, and single crochet back around to the other side, and join with a slip stitch. Chain 1, turn, and single crochet back to the beginning, joining with a slip stitch. Chain 1, turn, and single crochet back to the other side, joining with a slip stitch.

When you are happy with the size of the base of your pouch, you are going to begin with the decrease row.

Chain 1, and single crochet in the first 4 stitches, then skip the next stitch. Single crochet in the next 4 stitches, and skip the next stitch. Single crochet in the next 4 stitches, and skip the next stitch. Repeat this around.

Work 1 more decrease row.

Now, continue to work your way up the side of the pouch, until you are happy with the overall size of the piece.

Chain 1, turn, and single crochet around the row, joining with a slip stitch. Chain 1, turn, and single crochet back around to the other side, and join with a slip stitch. Chain 1, turn, and single crochet back to the beginning, joining with a slip stitch. Chain 1, turn, and single crochet back to the other side, joining with a slip stitch.

When you have the right size, tie off.

Take a length of yarn and feed it through the top portion of the pouch. Pull this tight to form the drawstring on the piece. You can add beads and lengths of yarn to the bottom of a more decorative effect. Tie off, and you are done!

The Catch All Crochet Bowl

Photo made by: <u>dainec</u>

You will need 1 skein of yarn in the color of your choice and a size J crochet hook

Chain 4 and join with a slip stitch to form a ring. Single crochet in the center of this ring 10 times, and join with a slip stitch.

Chain 1, turn, and single crochet around the row, joining with a slip stitch. Chain 1, turn, and single crochet back around to the other side, and join with a slip stitch. Chain 1, turn, and single crochet back to the beginning, joining with a slip stitch. Chain 1, turn, and single crochet back to the other side, joining with a slip stitch.

Chain 1, turn, and single crochet around the row, joining with a slip stitch. Chain 1, turn, and single crochet back around to the other side, and join with a slip stitch. Chain 1, turn, and single crochet back to the beginning, joining with a slip stitch. Chain 1, turn, and single crochet back to the other side, joining with a slip stitch.

When you are happy with the size of the base of the bowl, you are going to begin with the decrease row.

Chain 1, and single crochet in the first 4 stitches, then skip the next stitch. Single crochet in the next 4 stitches, and skip the next stitch. Single crochet in the next 4 stitches, and skip the next stitch. Repeat this around.

One decrease row is fine, as you want this to fan out rather than move straight up the side of the bowl.

Now, continue to work your way up the side of the bowl, until you are happy with the overall size of the piece.

Chain 1, turn, and single crochet around the row, joining with a slip stitch. Chain 1, turn, and single crochet back around to the other side, and join with a slip stitch. Chain 1, turn, and single crochet back to the beginning, joining with a slip stitch. Chain 1, turn, and single crochet back to the other side, joining with a slip stitch.

Change colors according to your preference, and when you are done, tie it off!

The Mandala Pendant

Photo made by: snarledskein

You will need 1 skein of yarn in the color of your choice and a size G crochet hook

Chain 4 and join with a slip stitch to form a ring. Single crochet in the center of this ring 10 times, and join with a slip stitch.

Chain 1, turn, and single crochet around the row, joining with a slip stitch. Chain 1, turn, and single crochet back around to the other side, and join with a slip stitch. Chain 1, turn, and single crochet back to the beginning, joining with a slip stitch. Chain 1, turn, and single crochet back to the other side, joining with a slip stitch.

Chain 1, turn, and single crochet around the row, joining with a slip stitch. Chain 1, turn, and single crochet back around to the other side, and join with a slip stitch. Chain 1, turn, and single crochet back to the beginning, joining with a slip stitch. Chain 1, turn, and single crochet back to the other side, joining with a slip stitch.

When you are happy with the size of the pendant, tie off.

Take your crochet hook and chain a length for the chain, and work 1 single crochet row across this piece. Tie off, and feed through the mandala pendant.

Secure the ends of the chain in place, and you are done!

Fruity Coasters

Photo made by: hellomomo

You will need 1 skein of yarn in the color of your choice and a size G crochet hook

Use the colors of your choice, or follow the colors listed above.

Chain 4 and join with a slip stitch to form a ring. Single crochet in the center of this ring 10 times, and join with a slip stitch.

Chain 1, turn, and single crochet around the row, joining with a slip stitch. Chain 1, turn, and single crochet back around to the other side, and join with a slip stitch. Chain 1, turn, and single crochet back to the beginning, joining with a slip stitch. Chain 1, turn, and single crochet back to the other side, joining with a slip stitch.

Chain 1, turn, and single crochet around the row, joining with a slip stitch. Chain 1, turn, and single crochet back around to the other side, and join with a slip stitch. Chain 1, turn, and single crochet back to the beginning, joining with a slip stitch. Chain 1, turn, and single crochet back to the other side, joining with a slip stitch.

When you are happy with the size of the coaster, tie off and set aside. Repeat for the other coasters, making each one the same size as the first coaster.

When you have finished, use green and chain a length of 10 stitches per piece. Sew this in place as you see in the photo, and your coasters are done!

The Coin Catcher

Photo made by: moonrat

You will need 1 skein of yarn in the color of your choice and a size G crochet hook

Chain 4 and join with a slip stitch to form a ring. Single crochet in the center of this ring 10 times, and join with a slip stitch.

Chain 1, turn, and single crochet around the row, joining with a slip stitch. Chain 1, turn, and single crochet back around to the other side, and join with a slip stitch. Chain 1, turn, and single crochet back to the beginning, joining with a slip stitch. Chain 1, turn, and single crochet back to the other side, joining with a slip stitch.

When you are happy with the size of the bottom of the bowl, you are going to begin with the decrease row.

Chain 1, and single crochet in the first 4 stitches, then skip the next stitch. Single crochet in the next 4 stitches, and skip the next stitch. Single crochet in the next 4 stitches, and skip the next stitch. Repeat this around.

Again, 1 decrease row is fine for a bowl, as you don't want it to go straight up, but rather fan out as you work.

Now, continue to work your way up the side of the bowl, until you are happy with the overall size of the piece.

Chain 1, turn, and single crochet around the row, joining with a slip stitch. Chain 1, turn, and single crochet back around to the other side, and join with a slip stitch. Chain 1, turn, and single crochet back to the beginning, joining with a slip stitch. Chain 1, turn, and single crochet back to the other side, joining with a slip stitch.

Tie off, and you are done!

Grass Is Always Greener Scarf

Photo made by: eldriva

You will need 1 skein of yarn in the green and a size J crochet hook

Chain a length that is 5 feet long.

Single crochet across the row. Chain 1, turn, and single crochet back to the beginning, in the front loop only. Chain 1, turn, and single crochet back to the other side of the row, again in the front loop only. Chain 1, turn, and single crochet across the row in the front loop only. Chain 1, turn, and single crochet back to the beginning in the front loop only.

Chain 1, turn, and single crochet across the row, in the front loop only. Chain 1, turn, and single crochet back to the beginning, in the front loop only. Chain 1, turn, and single crochet back to the other side of the row, again in the front loop only. Chain 1, turn, and single crochet across the row in the front loop only. Chain 1, turn, and single crochet back to the beginning in the front loop only.

Chain 1, turn, and single crochet across the row, in the front loop only. Chain 1, turn, and single crochet back to the beginning, in the front loop only. Chain 1, turn, and single crochet back to the other side of the row, again in the front loop only. Chain 1, turn, and single crochet across the row in the front loop only. Chain 1, turn, and single crochet back to the beginning in the front loop only.

Tie off.

Cut a fistful of yarn that is the same length (about 5 inches long.) Using your yarn needle or crochet hook, feed these lengths through the ends of the scarf, creating the fringe as you see in the photo. Continue until the fringe is as thick as you like, then take your scissors and cut it all down to the same length.

That's it! Your scarf is done!

Fast and Easy Dish Scrubby

Photo made by: <u>dainec</u>

You will need 1 skein of cotton yarn in the color of your choice and a size G crochet hook

Chain 4 and join with a slip stitch to form a ring. Single crochet in the center of this ring 10 times, and join with a slip stitch.

Chain 1, turn, and single crochet around the row, joining with a slip stitch. Chain 1, turn, and single crochet back around to the other side, and join with a slip stitch. Chain 1, turn, and single crochet back to the beginning, joining with a slip stitch. Chain 1, turn, and single crochet back to the other side, joining with a slip stitch.

Chain 1, turn, and single crochet around the row, joining with a slip stitch. Chain 1, turn, and single crochet back around to the other side, and join with a slip stitch. Chain 1, turn, and single crochet back to the beginning, joining with a slip stitch. Chain 1, turn, and single crochet back to the other side, joining with a slip stitch.

Continue until you are happy with the size of the scrubby – when it fits comfortably in your hand you are ready to tie off.

Tie off, and you are done!

Insider's Tip:

If you use hemp along with your yarn as you crochet, you will maximize the scrubbing power.

Mother's Favorite Washcloth

Photo made by: smittenkittenoriginals

You will need 1 skein of cotton yarn in the color of your choice and a size J crochet hook

Chain a length that is 6 inches long.

Single crochet across the row. Chain 1, turn, and single crochet back to the beginning. Chain 1, turn, and single crochet across the row. Chain 1, turn, and single crochet back to the beginning. Chain 1, turn, and single crochet across the row. Chain 1, turn, and single crochet back to the beginning.

Single crochet across the row. Chain 1, turn, and single crochet back to the beginning. Chain 1, turn, and single crochet across the row. Chain 1, turn, and single crochet back to the beginning. Chain 1, turn, and single crochet across the row. Chain 1, turn, and single crochet back to the beginning.

Single crochet across the row. Chain 1, turn, and single crochet back to the beginning. Chain 1, turn, and single crochet across the row. Chain 1, turn, and single crochet back to the beginning. Chain 1, turn, and single crochet across the row. Chain 1, turn, and single crochet back to the beginning.

When you have a square, tie off. You can create a single crochet border around the piece, or you can leave it as it is. Either way, your new washcloth is ready for anything!

Chunky Crochet Beanie

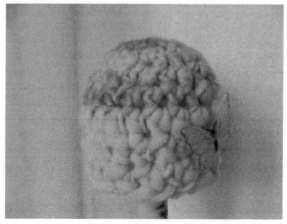

Photo made by: ilashdesigns

You will need 1 skein of chunky yarn in the color of your choice and a size J crochet hook

Chain 4 and join with a slip stitch to form a ring. Single crochet in the center of this ring 10 times, and join with a slip stitch.

Chain 1, turn, and single crochet around the row, joining with a slip stitch. Chain 1, turn, and single crochet back around to the other side, and join with a slip stitch. Chain 1, turn, and single crochet back to the beginning, joining with a slip stitch. Chain 1, turn, and single crochet back to the other side, joining with a slip stitch.

Chain 1, turn, and single crochet around the row, joining with a slip stitch. Chain 1, turn, and single crochet back around to the other side, and join with a slip stitch. Chain 1, turn, and single crochet back to the beginning, joining with a slip stitch. Chain 1, turn, and single crochet back to the other side, joining with a slip stitch.

When the hat can cover the top of your head, you are ready to decrease.

Chain 1, and single crochet in the first 4 stitches, then skip the next stitch. Single crochet in the next 4 stitches, and skip the next stitch. Single crochet in the next 4 stitches, and skip the next stitch. Repeat this around.

Work 1 more decrease row.

Now, continue to work your way around the hat, until you are happy with how it fits.

Chain 1, turn, and single crochet around the row, joining with a slip stitch. Chain 1, turn, and single crochet back around to the other side, and join with a slip stitch. Chain 1, turn, and single crochet back to the beginning, joining with a slip stitch. Chain 1, turn, and single crochet back to the other side, joining with a slip stitch.

Try it on as you go, and crochet it to fit your head. When you are happy with the size, tie off and you are done!

Conclusion

There you have it, a variety of adorable crochet projects you can make in just one hour. I know you love to crochet, but crochet can also take an incredibly long time to do, especially if you don't have a lot of time. I hope this book was able to give you the inspiration you need to create a variety of your own crochet projects, and that you create each and every one to be just what you want it to be.

You know you love to sit back and relax, and this book is going to give you the projects you need to make something in just a short amount of time. Let creativity flow, and have fun while you relax.

Happy crocheting!

Printed in Great Britain
by Amazon

36156046R00115